CANCELLED

# JULIUS CAESAR

D0706269

Did Caesar destroy the republic? What were the legality of his position and the moral justification for his actions? How good a general really was he? What was his relationship with Cleopatra? Why was he assassinated? What happened next?

Julius Caesar was a brilliant politician who became sole ruler of a Roman empire increased in size by his own military exploits. As a military strategist he never lost a campaign; he was also a considerable speaker and historical writer. A lavish spender, who at the outset of his career was often hugely in debt, he had by his death amassed by various means a personal fortune estimated as equal to one-seventh of the entire Roman treasury. His influence was profound and his sexual habits were the scandal of the age.

Antony Kamm provides a fresh account, for the general reader and the student, of Caesar's life, set against the historical, political, and social background of the times, with new translations from classical sources. Also featured are key figures such as Marius, Sulla, Cicero, Catiline, Pompey, Cato, Crassus, Clodius, Mark Antony, Servilia and her son Brutus, Gaius Octavius, who became the emperor Augustus, and his sister Octavia, Calpurnius Piso and his daughter Calpurnia (Caesar's wife), and Cleopatra, as well as the politicians who supported or opposed him and the military men who fought for and against him. For those people interested in the end of the Roman republic and the growth of the Roman empire, and the great figures of Roman history, this new look at an extraordinary man will be indispensable.

**Antony Kamm** read Classics and English at Oxford University. He was lecturer in publishing studies at the University of Stirling 1988–95. His publications include *Collins Biographical Dictionary of English Literature* (1993), *The Romans: an introduction* (Routledge, 1995), *The Israelites: an introduction* (Routledge, 1999), *Julius Caesar: a beginner's guide* (2002), *The Last Frontier: the Roman invasions of Scotland* (2004), and for children, *Scotland in Roman Times* (1998).

# JULIUS CAESAR

## A life

*Antony Kamm*

Routledge
Taylor & Francis Group

LONDON AND NEW YORK

ROCKY RIVER PUBLIC LIBRARY
1600 Hampton Road • Rocky River, OH 44116

First published 2006
by Routledge
2 Park Square, Milton Park, Abingdon, Oxon OX14 4RN

Simultaneously published in the USA and Canada
by Routledge
270 Madison Avenue, New York, NY 10016

*Routledge is an imprint of the Taylor & Francis Group, an informa business*

© 2006 Antony Kamm
Line drawings by Jennifer Campbell
Copyright © Jennifer Campbell 2005

Typeset in Garamond 3 by
RefineCatch Limited, Bungay, Suffolk
Printed and bound in Great Britain by
Antony Rowe Ltd, Chippenham, Wiltshire

All rights reserved. No part of this book may be reprinted or
reproduced or utilized in any form or by any electronic,
mechanical, or other means, now known or hereafter
invented, including photocopying and recording, or in any
information storage or retrieval system, without permission
in writing from the publishers.

*British Library Cataloguing in Publication Data*
A catalogue record for this book is available from the British Library

*Library of Congress Cataloging in Publication Data*
Kamm, Antony.
Julius Caesar / Antony Kamm.
p. cm.
Includes bibliographical references and index.
1. Caesar, Julius. 2. Rome—History—Republic, 265–30 B.C.
3. Heads of state—Rome—Biography. 4. Generals—Rome—
Biography. I. Title.
DG261.K36 2006
937′.05092—dc22
2005036603

ISBN10: 0–415–36415–9 (hbk)
ISBN10: 0–415–41121–1 (pbk)
ISBN10: 0–203–01534–7 (ebk)

ISBN13: 978–0–415–36415–7 (hbk)
ISBN13: 978–0–415–41121–9 (pbk)
ISBN13: 978–0–203–01534–6 (ebk)

ROCKY RIVER PUBLIC LIBRARY

3 3189 00731549 4

For

DERRY JEFFARES

(1920–2005)

academic, friend, and mentor

# CONTENTS

*List of figures*                                            ix
*List of plans*                                              x
*Acknowledgements*                                           xi
*Map 1: Italy*                                               xii
*Map 2: The Mediterranean*                                   xiii
*Map 3: Gaul and southern Britain*                           xiv
*Map 4: Greece*                                              xv

Prologue: January 49 BC                                      1

1  The world of republican Rome                              3

2  The man in the making 100–73 BC                           19

3  The politician 73–63 BC                                   36

4  Praetor and consul 62–59 BC                               48

5  The general: Gaul and Britain 58–55 BC                    62

6  The general: Britain to the Rubicon 54–49 BC              80

7  The dictator: Civil War 49–48 BC                          101

8  Egyptian interlude 48–47 BC                               115

9  The dictator: Civil War 47–45 BC                          125

10  The Ides of March 44 BC                                  139

11 Epilogue 44–27 BC                                             152


*Genealogical chart of the family of Julius Caesar*                156
*Simplified genealogical chart of the emperors from Augustus*
   *to Nero*                                                      157
*Table of dates*                                                  158
*Principal sources*                                               160
*Index*                                                          163

# FIGURES

| | | |
|---|---|---|
| 1.1 | Senators | 6 |
| 2.1 | Family group | 21 |
| 2.2 | Coin depicting Sulla | 26 |
| 3.1 | Priests | 45 |
| 6.1 | Coin of Caesar 49 BC | 85 |
| 6.2 | Coin depicting prisoner representing Gaul | 87 |
| 6.3 | Coin possibly depicting Vercingetorix | 89 |
| 7.1 | Head of Pompey | 104 |
| 8.1 | Head of Caesar from Egypt | 122 |
| 9.1 | Bust of Caesar | 133 |
| 10.1 | Coin of Caesar 44 BC | 143 |
| 10.2 | Coin depicting Lucius Junius Brutus | 146 |
| 10.3 | Bust of Gaius Octavius | 150 |
| 11.1 | The Ides of March! | 154 |

# PLANS

Plan 1: The battle of Bibracte 58 BC     67
Plan 2: The action at Gergovia 52 BC     91
Plan 3: The siege of Alesia 52 BC     94
Plan 4: Dyrrachium 48 BC     110
Plan 5: The battle of Pharsalus 48 BC     113
Plan 6: Alexandria 48–47 BC     119

# ACKNOWLEDGEMENTS

The starting point for this book was the short introduction, *Julius Caesar: a beginner's guide*, published by Hodder and Stoughton in 2002 and now out of print. I am grateful to Dr Barbara Levick for her comments on that book, which have been taken into account in preparing this revised, recast, and much extended version. Particular thanks are due to Dr\u00aa Gisela Negrão Neto for advice on medical and other matters, and for the suggestion that Cleopatra may have brought to Rome as a gift the statue of herself that Caesar caused to be set up in the temple of Venus Genetrix. I also gladly acknowledge points raised in the pseudonymous discussions of the Aedes Divi Julii group of the Ancient Worlds web site which have found their way into my text.

I was much saddened by the death in 2004 of Michael Dixon, a widely travelled and knowledgeable photographer who was also a good friend. Through the offices of his wife Mary, responsibility for his photographic library has now been undertaken by the Ancient Art & Architecture Collection, whose staff members Etty Morris and Haruko Sheridan have been most helpful in meeting my requests for his pictures and those of other photographers. All the coin images are copyright the Hunterian Museum and Art Gallery, University of Glasgow, for whom Iona Shepherd gave me every assistance. The coins themselves are from the Hunterian's collection, to whose curator, Dr Donal Bateson, I am grateful for his help in selection and captioning.

It would be virtually impossible for me to write a book of this nature without the resources and services of Stirling University Library. Jennifer Campbell has brought skills practised over many years to the task of recreating, as chapter-head drawings, the features of some of the key players in the story.

My thanks are due once again to my publisher, Richard Stoneman, for his wisdom and encouragement. Matthew Gibbons, assistant editor, has been a vital source of information on editorial and technical matters. The book has benefited considerably from the experience and understanding of Katherine Davey as production editor, and from the sympathetic copy editing of Jackie Dias and the proof-reading of Carol Fellingham Webb.

A. K.

*Map 1* Italy

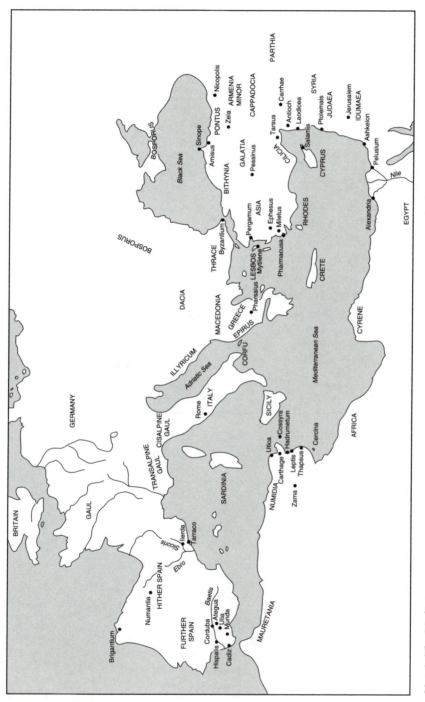

*Map 2* The Mediterranean

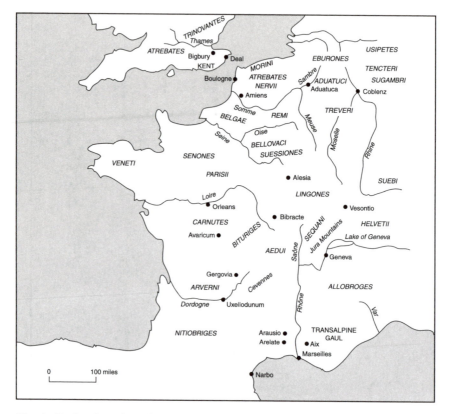

*Map 3* Gaul and southern Britain

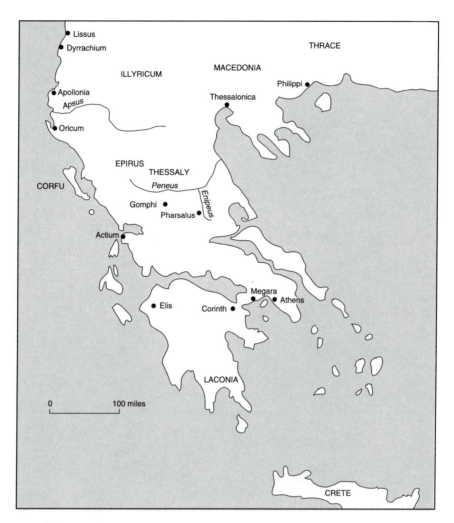

*Map 4* Greece

# PROLOGUE
## January 49 BC

So when it was reported to Caesar [in Cisalpine Gaul] that the tribunes' veto had been rejected, and that they had left Rome, he immediately sent several cohorts ahead secretly. He himself, so as not to arouse suspicion, concealed his intentions by attending a public stage performance, inspecting the plans of a training school for gladiators that he was sponsoring, and dining as usual with a crowd of hangers-on. Then, after sunset, he set out silently, with a small escort, in a carriage drawn by mules commandeered from a local bakery. His lights failed, he lost the way, and he blundered about until at last at dawn, having found someone to give directions, he finished the journey on foot along barely discernible paths.

Having caught up with the cohorts at the river Rubicon, which marked the boundary of his province, he stopped for a moment, and reflected on the enormity of what he was about to do. Then he turned to those around him: 'We can still go back,' he said. 'But once we cross that little bridge, it will be fighting all the way!'

While he paused, as though in doubt, there came a sign. A huge, magnificent presence suddenly materialized close by, sitting down and playing on a pipe. When not only shepherds flocked around to listen, but also soldiers, among whom were several trumpeters, left their posts to join the audience, the apparition snatched an instrument from one of them, ran to the river, sounded the advance with a tremendous blast, and crossed over to the other side.

At that, Caesar cried, 'Let us go, where the signs of the gods and the unjust cause of our enemies call us! The die is cast.'

Suetonius, *Julius Caesar* 31–3

MARIUS

# 1

# THE WORLD OF REPUBLICAN ROME

> So, in those former times the senate administered the constitu-
> tion in such a way that though the populace was free, little
> public business was done by the people, but much by authority
> of the senate, according to established precedent. Moreover,
> though the consuls held office for only one year, their power
> was in effect and in law that of kings, and to ensure that the
> influence of the nobility was maintained, the principle was
> firmly upheld that no business of a popular assembly could be
> ratified without the approval of the senate.
>
> Cicero, *On the Republic* II. 56

Julius Caesar did not destroy the Roman republic, so much as play a starring
role in its obsequies. He was an idealist, a workaholic, and a political enabler
and manipulator, who would bend the system to his own ends if the wheels
of change did not whirl fast enough for him. As things turned out, his
autocratic attitude and his preoccupation with quick results were the principal reasons for his assassination, which signalled the bloodstained dawn of
the new era of imperial Rome.

By the first century BC, the traditional distinction between the patricians
(members of a group of ancient, aristocratic families) and the plebs (the

3

people, that is the rest of the community) had largely disappeared. The new ruling class comprised the 'nobility', a status automatically assumed by patricians and by descendants of former consuls but which could be acquired, as it was by Cicero himself, by achieving the consulship. Members of the nobility exercised their power by means of arrogance, wealth, intrigue, and patronage. Patronage imposed a legal as well as a moral obligation to help one's clients; its philosophy survives in the public arena today in the state's provision of legal aid. The nobility effectively controlled the senate and, through their strings of clients, the election of officers of state. These officers included the holders of religious posts (the members of the priestly colleges and the *pontifex maximus* himself), all of whom were political appointees. It was nepotism on a grand scale.

Cicero was Caesar's political, literary, and forensic contemporary; his ideal constitution, if it ever existed, failed to take into account various other destabilizing influences. While allowing for the overriding influence of the nobility and of the senate, he ignored the existence of the class of citizens known as *equites*, or equestrians. These men, originally numbering about 1800, were, by reason of their property holding, until the second century BC provided at public expense with a horse, with which they were required to report for military duty. Now, their numbers bolstered by anyone else qualified by wealth and by senators' sons, the *equites* represented a considerable political power grouping which ranked just below the six hundred or so senators. Since senators were forbidden by law to participate in trade, the *equites* incorporated the entire commercial elite of Rome.

In the home and in the fields, gods and goddesses presided over the activities of daily life, while the superstitions of the religion of the state pervaded military action as well as the conduct of public business. Armies would take along with them a portable auspice-kit in the form of a cage of sacred chickens. It was a bad sign if the chickens refused to eat offerings of cake. If they ate them and let grains fall from their beaks, the omens for battle were good. Memories of national disaster died hard in the Roman world. When in 216 BC Hannibal the Carthaginian was ensconced in Italy with only a small army, the Romans, who easily outnumbered his force, were still hesitant about being brought to battle. The chickens were duly consulted, and declined their food. Both consuls in charge of the Roman army, Gaius Terentius Varro and Lucius Aemilius Paullus, called to mind their unfortunate predecessor, Publius Claudius Pulcher. In 249 BC, Pulcher had begun a sea-battle against the Carthaginians although the chickens had refused to eat; not only that, but he had thrown the chickens into the sea, remarking that if they would not eat, they could drink. He lost the battle, and with it 93 ships and their crews, captured by the Carthaginians. Ignoring this dire precedent, however, Varro, whose turn of command it was on that particular day, led the Roman army, at Cannae, to one of the greatest defeats in its history.

Omens controlled the affairs, too, of the senate and other assemblies. In

59 BC, Caesar's consular colleague, Marcus Calpurnius Bibulus, opposed most of his measures on principle. Bibulus's well-tried tactics were to object on religious grounds to the assemblies sitting. When Caesar took no notice, Bibulus interrupted the public meeting which his colleague was addressing from the steps of the temple of Castor, and tried to make himself heard. Caesar's hired hands, some of whom were armed, pelted him with dung and beat up his officials.

Fearing for his life, Bibulus barricaded himself in his house, which he did not leave during his remaining eight months of office. Instead, he sent messages to say that he was examining the sky for omens. Any announcement of unfavourable omens had to be made personally before the business of the day began. Bibulus could not do so without risking bodily harm. Was this justified cause for not appearing in person? Nobody was sure. Caesar's measures were approved, but doubts were sown as to whether they were legal.

The Latin term *res publica* (matters of public concern), also as one word *respublica*, is usually translated as state or commonwealth; from it, via the French, comes the English word 'republic'. The Roman republic was never a democracy in the true Greek sense, with everyone in theory having an equal say. The history of Rome during the latter years of the republic is, in the same way as modern politics, all about power. The Romans had a precise word, *imperium*, of which a literal translation is something between power and command. It is related to *imperator*, the title bestowed on a victorious military commander by his troops; from it derive the terms 'empire' and 'emperor'.

The two consuls were invested by right with *imperium* during their year of office, as to a lesser degree were the praetors, officers of state who ranked immediately below the consuls. *Imperium* could be extended for further terms in the case of provincial governors and military commanders, who were former consuls or praetors, appointed by the senate. The office of censor, of which there were two, was usually reserved for those who had achieved all the steps on the political ladder or *cursus honorum* (the race, or course, of honours) from quaestor to consul. Censors were chief registrars, finance and tax officers, inspectors of public works, and governors of public morality. Elections were held every five years, to coincide with the census of the people. The censors, who had wide disciplinary powers, served in office for only 18 months, but their acts remained in force until the next election.

The senate was primarily a consultative body. As a general rule, its members discussed and voted on matters put to them by the presiding officer, but the results of their deliberations had no legal force. They had, however, overriding responsibility for the administration of the state and its empire, finance, and relations with foreign powers.

Outside the senate, a unique system of voting kept the decision-making largely in the hands of those who wielded most power, or commanded most money. The assembly known as the *comitia centuriata* elected senior state

*Figure 1.1* A group of Roman senators of the first century BC, from the *Ara Pacis* (Altar of Peace), completed in 12 BC. (C. M. Dixon/Ancient Art & Architecture Collection)

officials, approved legislation, and decided in cases of offences against the state for which the punishment was death or exile. It comprised all Roman citizens, who were allocated to one of 193 centuries according to their means. A century comprised an indefinite and variable number of members, each of whom had one vote. The larger the century, the less was the influence of a single vote, and a simple majority governed the way in which that century would cast its vote on the issue under discussion or on the election of an official. Where the system favoured the rich and the influential was that 98 of the votes (that is, a majority) were in the hands of the 18 centuries of equestrians and the 80 representing the top of the five property bands.

The *comitia tributa* (tribal assembly) was also open to all citizens, and voted according to 35 tribal or district divisions. It elected minor officials and approved legislation on a different voting basis to that of the *comitia centuriata*.

The functions of the *comitia curiata*, an assembly of representatives of wards, ten each from the original three tribes of Rome, were largely, after the fourth century BC, assumed by the *comitia centuriata*, but not before there had been a dramatic interruption of its business. By ancient tradition, the Roman constitution had allowed for the appointment in times of national emergency of a single 'dictator' (the term, in Latin, means commander, someone who gives orders), to exercise complete control, with overriding *imperium*, for not

6

more than six months. His second-in-command, even in late republican times, was called 'master of the cavalry'. In 310 BC, Lucius Papirius was appointed dictator to combat the continuing menace of the Samnites. He was in the process of asking the *comitia curiata* to go through the formality of ratifying his nomination of Bubulcus as master of the cavalry, when it was noticed that it was curia Faucia's turn to vote first. This was a sinister omen, because on two earlier occasions when this had happened, the consequence was disastrous to the state. Papirius cancelled the vote, and took it again the next day, with a favourable outcome and a successful conclusion to his campaign.

The people's right to the highest office was accepted in 367 BC, after which one consul was normally a plebeian. The people's right to improve their lot was achieved at an even earlier stage, not by violence, but by passive resistance and collective bargaining. There arose out of this the *concilium plebis* (people's assembly), with authority to enact legislation which, after 287 BC, could, with the approval of the senate, that is to say if the omens were favourable, be made binding on the whole community. The *concilium plebis* became the most convenient channel for the passage of legislation, largely for technical reasons, since its religious procedures were less complicated and less formal than those of the other assemblies. Its own elected officers, the tribunes of the people, had the power to veto any measure proposed by an officer of state (including a consul) or by another tribune which appeared to contravene the law or the established conduct of elections. It was a tool open to the most flagrant misuse.

The political system began seriously to unravel during the events of 133 BC, at a time when a further division of alignments is discernible: between the *populares*, whose political aims were achieved by appealing to the people, and the *optimates*, whose inclination was to preserve the *status quo*.

The brothers Gracchus, Tiberius (b. 163 BC) and Gaius (b. 154 BC), were nobles, in that they were the sons of a former consul and the grandsons, through their mother, of the distinguished general Publius Cornelius Scipio Africanus, who was twice consul. They were also *populares* of a genuine crusading nature.

Tiberius Sempronius Gracchus, elected tribune of the people for 133 BC, proposed an agrarian law whereby large tracts of land acquired by the state in its conquests of Italy should be redistributed to needy smallholders, with guaranteed tenure in return for a nominal rent. The present occupants, who were tenants of the state, were to be restricted to what was nominally the legal limit of 500 Roman acres of public land, plus 250 acres for each of up to two sons, and would be compensated by the grant of a hereditary rent-free lease. It was a significant package of measures, at a time of general expansion abroad, which also restored to the list of those eligible for military service, who traditionally qualified by owning property, a section of society which had become ineligible. The bill was drafted with the help of consultants who included Publius Mucius Scaevola, consul for that year and a noted legal expert, and Licinius Crassus Mucianus, a distinguished lawyer who was also the father-in-law of Gaius Sempronius Gracchus.

Objections were expected from large landowners who had invested money in the development of their estates, many of whom were senators. Tiberius, however, through his family and other connections, could command support in the senate, including that of his father-in-law, Appius Claudius Pulcher, father of the house. So determined was he, though, to get the measures passed without interminable discussion, that he resorted to questionable tactics. Relying on a hundred-year-old precedent, instead of submitting his bill first to the senate, he arranged to propose it direct to the *concilium plebis*, where it was bound to be accepted without ado. Members of the senate, outraged at their traditional rights being infringed, prevailed upon Marcus Octavius, one of the other tribunes, to veto the bill as it was being read out, which he was entitled to do. Tiberius, having failed to persuade Marcus Octavius to withdraw the veto, flatly refused to refer the issue to the senate. He then took the unprecedented step of calling on the assembly to vote his refractory colleague out of office, which it did. The bill was then approved with acclamation, and, at Tiberius's suggestion, an independent commission was established to administer it, consisting of himself, his brother, and his father-in-law.

The senate tried to block the commission's activities by allocating from the public treasury a derisory sum as funding. Tiberius coolly proposed to the *concilium plebis* that part of the expected inheritance by Rome of the estate of the late king of Pergamum, of which, through his family connections, he had advance knowledge, should be diverted to the commission's use. This measure, unsurprisingly, was passed too.

The senate had now been outmanoeuvred in two areas which it regarded as its prerogative, finance and foreign policy. There were also suggestions that by manipulating the process of law, packing a commission with members of his family, removing a colleague from office, and appropriating public money for his own purposes, Tiberius Gracchus was setting himself up as some kind of king. He was now a marked man.

State officials could not be prosecuted during their term of office, but a prosecution could not be avoided by moving directly to another post. Tiberius announced that he was standing for the tribuneship for a second term, which was unprecedented if not strictly illegal. When he and his supporters gathered on the Capitol Hill, where the assembly met and where the elections were due to be held, a group of senators, led by Publius Scipio Nasica, the *pontifex maximus*, charged out of the senate house and clubbed to death Tiberius and 200 of his followers. That night the bodies were unceremoniously thrown into the river Tiber.

This eruption of political violence echoed down the years; 80 years later, politically motivated thuggery and gang warfare had become commonplace in the streets. Further retaliation against Tiberius Gracchus's supporters was taken in 132 BC by the consuls for that year, who used legal procedures to circumvent the traditional right of the people to pass judgment on those found guilty of plotting to overthrow the state, and in this way were able to sentence them to permanent exile.

Notwithstanding these open expressions of opposition, the work of the land commission continued, with Tiberius Gracchus being replaced by Licinius Crassus Mucianus. Gaius Gracchus, who clearly harboured deep resentment at the treatment of his brother, was biding his time. He was more flamboyant and passionate than Tiberius, but he was methodical in the planning and exercise of his political career, and he was a formidable public speaker. It was not until 126 BC that he offered himself for public office as quaestor, when he was about three years over the minimum age. The post principally involved acting as assistant to the consuls, and it was in this capacity that he served as military aide to the consul Aurelius Orestes in Sardinia, which had been annexed in 241 BC at the end of the First Punic War against Carthage and was one of the earliest provinces of the Roman empire. They were still there in 124 BC, when Gaius returned to Rome, presumably with Orestes's permission, to stand as tribune of the people. While the votes in the assembly placed him fourth out of the ten tribunes elected, it was clear that he commanded considerable support from the public itself.

Gaius Gracchus was 30 when he took office as tribune. By some means he managed to be elected in 123 BC for a second term; it appears that he may have taken advantage of a constitutional loophole whereby if there were not enough candidates for election, the people might choose further tribunes from the whole body of citizens. For breadth and imaginative scope, the measures that he introduced during those two years were unmatched until Julius Caesar's energetic dictatorship between 49 and 44 BC, when Caesar was in his early fifties. Gaius's acts and actions benefited everybody but the aristocracy and the senate, for which institution he maintained an open contempt.

One of his earliest measures was a retrospective law establishing beyond doubt that cases for which the punishment was execution or exile were the prerogative of the people, represented by the *comitia centuriata*, and quashing all previous unauthorized sentences. By it, all supporters of Tiberius Gracchus effectively received pardons, and the surviving consul for 132 BC, Popillius Laenas, was himself forced into exile.

Gaius removed the privilege of the senate to try fellow-senators for extortion as provincial governors, and handed it over to juries comprised exclusively of equestrians. Provincial governors were former consuls or praetors, and the opportunities for personal enrichment were legendary. Gaius restricted the traditional policy of the senate to reward favoured consuls with the richest pickings, by insisting that the choice of provinces be made before

9

the elections for consul were held. He increased the potential wealth of the equestrian order by transferring responsibility for auctioning the contracts for collecting taxes in the province of Asia from the governor on the spot to the appropriate officials in Rome. He also embarked on an extensive programme of building roads and constructing new granaries, to the benefit of equestrians who won the contracts for these.

The granaries were for storing the state's supplies of grain, which, under Gaius's new corn law, were made available for the people of Rome to buy at a fixed rate. He looked at terms of service in the army, re-establishing 17 as the minimum age of entry, and making the state responsible for supplying weapons and uniform. He gave authority for new self-governing colonies to be established in Italy, with plots of land for the urban poor. He also proposed that a new colony be founded on the site of Carthage, the once-proud city which the Romans, as a symbolic gesture of mastery, had reduced to rubble at the end of the Third Punic War in 146 BC, selling off into slavery the 50,000 men, women, and children who had survived the siege.

Gaius Gracchus's most enlightened legislative innovation, however, fell foul even of the *concilium plebis*. Since the beginning of the second century BC, the whole of Italy had been under Roman control. The nature of the rule of Rome over the various peoples and regions of Italy was dictated by the circumstances and by the observance of the Latin proverb, '*Divide et impera* (Divide and rule)', though all had regularly to provide troops to fight in the armies of the empire. Now, Gaius had proposed that the population of Latium, which enclosed the city of Rome, should be granted full Roman citizenship, and that the rest of Italy should be allowed the preferential rights at present enjoyed by the Latins. Appian of Alexandria, the second-century AD historian, who wrote a history of Rome in Greek, suggests that Gaius proposed giving voting rights to all inhabitants of Italy.

Gaius's position was further undermined by the tactics of another tribune, Livius Drusus, who was obviously a tool of the senate. Livius used his powers of veto sparingly but tellingly, and also capped some of Gaius's proposals by putting forward more ambitious, but fallacious, measures of his own.

The Carthaginian settlement was to be called Junonia, after the Roman goddess Juno. In 122 BC Gaius unwisely abandoned his post as tribune in order to go to Carthage to lay out the foundations of the colony. This was an unprecedented step, as tribunes of the people were normally required to be on call to any citizen day and night, and were not allowed to leave Rome for more than a day. He was away for 70 days. On his return he unsuccessfully sought election for a third term.

Gaius was now without public office, but not without public support. When the administration for 121 BC started to dismantle his measures, and proposed to revoke even the establishment of Junonia, Gaius and his followers arrived at the meeting in force. There was an incident, and a bystander was killed. One of the consuls for that year, Lucius Opimius, who was overtly and viciously opposed to Gaius, used his influence to promulgate a decree, later known as a *senatus consultum ultimum*, which in effect gave backing to a senior official to take armed action against those who were endangering the stability of the state. Gaius escaped the first wave of violence, but then, realizing that the position was hopeless, ordered a slave to stab him to death. Opimius had 3000 of Gaius's supporters rounded up and put in jail, where they were systematically strangled.

The fates of the brothers Gracchus foreshadowed the demise of the Roman republic. A remarkable person, strong willed and with firmly set goals, can alter the direction of a nation, for better or for worse. Rome now had three such men in quick succession: Gaius Marius (157–86 BC), Lucius Cornelius Sulla (138–78 BC), and Julius Caesar (100–44 BC).

Gaius Marius was born near Arpinum, a town in Latium about 60 miles from Rome, not far off the Via Latina, the main road to Capua. Politically, he was *novus homo* (a new man, or upstart), the strict meaning of which is the first in his family to attain the post of consul. He was also regarded as something of a country bumpkin. Velleius Paterculus (19 BC–after AD 31), historian of Rome, wrote: '[Marius was] a countryman by birth, an uncouth, unpolished ascetic, eminent as a soldier but out of his depth in time of peace, immensely ambitious, never fulfilled, headstrong, and hyperactive' (II. 11). Though Marius's family was of equestrian rank, and clients of the Metelli, a distinguished family of the plebeian nobility who could boast several consuls in each generation, he never himself denied his rustic origins. Indeed, he tended to glory in them:

> 'People criticize me for my low birth and uncouth ways; because I don't give tasteful enough dinner parties, or have a clown, or a cook for whom I paid more than for my steward. Which, fellow citizens, I freely acknowledge. For I learned from my father, and from other admirable men, that elegance is a woman's prerogative, hard work a man's.'
>
> Sallust, *Jugurthan War* 90

As a soldier, he served in Spain in the army which blockaded and after nine years finally caused the defeat of the town of Numantia in 133 BC. With the help of the Metellus family, he was elected a tribune of the people for 119 BC, during which the consuls were Lucius Aurelius Cotta and Lucius Caecilius Metellus Delmaticus. He pleased members of the senate by opposing the extension of the corn distribution. He then displeased them by introducing a measure designed to nullify a proposal to narrow the bridges crossed by members of the *comitia tributa* in order to register their votes, thus increasing opportunities for intimidation. He also offended the Metelli, for when commanded by the senate to justify his action, he threatened to have both consuls arrested.

11

Marius subsequently stood for election as aedile, the next step up from quaestor. There were two grades of aedile, the senior one being known as curule aedile; *sella curulis* (curule chair), a cushioned stool with curved ivory legs, was the official seat of consuls, praetors (the next step after aedile), and senior aediles. When it looked as though he had no hope of being elected curule aedile, Marius changed his candidature, stood for the junior grade, and failed again. Nothing daunted, in 115 BC he offered himself for election as praetor. He got in this time, but was last of the successful candidates, and was then accused of cheating at the polls. He was acquitted on a technicality, the jury's votes being equally divided.

After an unmemorable year of office, he served as governor of the province of Further Spain, where he dealt with some minor disturbances and modestly lined his pockets. On his return to Rome he, perhaps wisely, made no attempt to stand for election as consul, which he was now qualified to do. He did, however, increase his social standing by marrying into the Julii, an upper-class family of illustrious origins but small material success, who claimed to be descended from Iulus, son of Aeneas, the mythical originator of city of Rome. Aeneas's father Anchises was mortal, but his mother was said to have been the goddess Venus.

Maybe Marius's new family connection stood him in good stead, for in 109 BC he was chosen by the consul for that year, Quintus Caecilius Metellus Numidicus (brother of the consul of 119 BC), to accompany him to Africa as a legionary commander. The assignment was to pursue the war against Jugurtha, which had dragged on since 113 BC amid accusations of incompetence and corruption on the part of the Roman command. Jugurtha, bequeathed one-third of the client-kingdom of Numidia by his adoptive father, had claimed all of it, having murdered the one and defeated the other of his co-legatees. A Roman client-kingdom was considered at that time a convenient way of keeping the peace in outposts of the empire where local knowledge and local methods of warfare were likely to be the most effective means. There was also, however, an obligation on Rome to intervene by taking diplomatic or military action in cases of internal unrest.

While still in Africa, Marius decided to stand as a candidate in the consular elections for the year 107 BC. Quintus Metellus refused to let him go. Marius retaliated by stirring up trouble within the army and in Rome, claiming that he could finish the war in half the time. He was allowed to return home, where his blunt, persuasive rhetoric won him the consulship by appealing both to equestrians and to the people, neither of which sections of society was keen on the war being extended for longer than was absolutely necessary. Having been elected consul constitutionally by the *comitia centuriata*, a precedent was now established which had far-reaching repercussions. The appointment to military commands was the prerogative of the senate, which now approved the extension of Quintus Metellus's assignment in Africa for a further year. The *comitia tributa*, however, overruled the resolution

12

by voting Marius into the job with immediate effect. Fifty years later the same means were employed to appoint Gnaeus Pompeius Magnus (Pompey the Great) and Julius Caesar to extraordinary commands, further weakening the influence of the senate along the road to the end of the republic.

The soil and climate of Italy offered prosperity to agriculturalists. Early Rome was forced into military campaigns of aggression simply to survive. Originally, armies consisted largely of peasant farmers. With Rome almost continually at war, there was no-one to tend the smallholdings, which fell into disuse. The Roman empire grew partly as a defensive measure and partly to enrich the economy. Tiberius Gracchus had tried to resolve the army recruitment problem at a time when the empire was beginning to expand into the lands round the Mediterranean, by creating more property owners. This increased the number of men eligible to serve in the army, but did nothing for the agricultural communities. As more and more men were conscripted from the land, produce from the new conquests enriched the equestrian entrepreneurs in Rome, who in turn invested in extensive agricultural estates managed by slave labour. The failed and dispossessed smallholders joined the ranks of the urban poor, known as the *capite censi* (registered by head count), who were ineligible for military service. There was now also the problem, which Pompey and Caesar would continually address, that with all this additional military activity, the soldier had nothing to which to return at the end of his service.

Marius was a professional military administrator as well as a soldier. He abandoned hundreds of years of tradition by enlisting the *capite censi*, with promises also of booty, glory, and permanent employment. Within a few years he revolutionized battle tactics, training methods, and mobility on the march. He instilled pride and loyalty into the troops by replacing the variety of emblems of a legion with the single eagle standard.

At the head, now, of an augmented, professional army, the first that Rome ever had, Marius with some difficulty brought an end to the African war. The *coup de grâce* for Jugurtha himself, however, was his betrayal by his father-in-law, the king of Mauretania. This was engineered by Marius's personal assistant, Lucius Cornelius Sulla, a quaestor now in his early thirties, who later felt that he should have got more credit for his contribution.

So popular was the victory, however, that the combined electorate of the *equites*, now able to resume their profitable African trade, and plebs voted Marius as consul for 104 BC while he was still in Numidia. This act of further defiance against the senate flouted a fifty-year-old law which prohibited the re-election of a consul within ten years of his previous term of office. With the post went the command of the army against the Germanic and Celtic tribes who had for some years been threatening the Roman province of Gallia Narbonensis (Transalpine Gaul), and even Italy itself. The trouble had started, as it so often did in the ancient world, with mass movements of folk seeking new homes. In this case it was the Germanic tribes from the vicinity of Jutland, the Teutones and Cimbri, trekking south with their families to escape inroads into their territories caused by the sea. On their way they disturbed the Celtic tribes of Gaul.

Between 109 and 105 BC the Romans had suffered four serious defeats in Gaul, culminating in the loss, it was said, of 80,000 men at Arausio (modern Orange), after the two Roman commanders, a patrician and a *novus homo*, had refused to co-operate with each other in the face of the combined forces of the Cimbri and Teutones.

Marius's appointment came when Italy effectively lay open to invasion from the north. By the time he returned to Rome in January 104, the Cimbri had taken themselves off to try their luck in Spain, and the Teutones were stirring things up in northern Gaul, both probably having decided that Rome was too tough a nut to crack on its home ground. This gave Marius time to enlist and train more troops, and somehow to persuade the electorate to extend his tenure of offices to cover the additional years 103, 102, and 101 BC. During this time he destroyed the Teutones at Aquae Sextiae (Aix) in 102 BC, and then in 101 BC at Vercellae, actually in Italy, he came to the rescue of his fellow consul of 102 BC, Q. Lutatius Catulus, and defeated the Cimbri, who had meanwhile returned to the hostilities. Between 65,000 and 100,000 Cimbri were killed, and the rest sold off to the slave dealers. Marius and Catulus were honoured by the senate with a joint triumph, though Marius ensured that, quite properly, he got most of the credit, offending Catulus in the process. Sulla, who was now serving as one of Catulus's legionary commanders, and who had subsequently driven off a half-hearted invasion of Italy from the eastern end of the Alps by the Tigurini, was also aggrieved, and there was now antagonism between the three men.

Consuls on campaign needed political cronies in Rome. Marius's particular abettor was Lucius Appuleius Saturninus, who had helped Marius to the consulship in 102 BC. Saturninus, who had been sacked by the senate from his post as quaestor in charge of corn supplies at Ostia, the port of Rome, was not above violence to achieve his political or personal ends. His election as tribune of the people for 103 BC and, after the murder of another candidate, again for 100 BC enhanced his usefulness to Marius, who needed another command, and land for his veterans to whom he had promised it; he also needed a foil for his bluff and unsophisticated approach to politics.

Marius was elected consul for yet another unprecedented term, his sixth, in 100 BC. Saturninus duly delivered his side of the bargain by introducing a package of laws in the Gracchus mould, among which were allotments for army veterans (including Latins and other Italians, some of whom would qualify for full Roman citizenship with voting rights), the foundation of overseas colonies, and mobilization to combat the pirates in the eastern Mediterranean – the implication was that this force would be commanded by Marius. In order to neutralize opposition from the senate, each law was equipped with an additional provision requiring senators to swear to observe it.

The urban mob reacted angrily to what they saw as preferential treatment for non-Romans; Saturninus called in a bunch of Marius's expectant veterans, who routed them with home-made cudgels. Marius, when publicly called upon by Saturninus to take the oaths of compliance with his measures, did so reluctantly, adding a carefully-phrased rider that he would obey them if they were indeed laws. The other senators followed suit, except for Quintus Metellus, who preferred to go into exile rather than contribute to public, and possibly violent, controversy.

Saturninus now overreached himself by adding murder to his stock in trade, when he procured the death in a riot of the political rival of a close associate. The senate responded with a *senatus consultum ultimum* requiring Marius to take action to secure the safety of the state. Saturninus and his followers occupied the Capitol building. Marius cut off the water supply, and forced them to surrender. Before the senate could decide on their fate, an angry crowd broke through the roof of the place in which they were being held, and stoned them to death with the tiles.

With the senate now declaring Saturninus's most recent legislation null and void, Marius's position became untenable, and he took an extended holiday abroad. A people's assembly had twice abrogated the traditional right of the senate to make senior military appointments; by refusing to acknowledge the soldier's right to a proper reward for his services, the senate had now lost all standing with the rank and file of the army. From now on, whoever commanded the army, commanded the state.

On his return to Rome, Marius built himself a house near the forum so as to make himself more available to those who came to pay their respects, and waited for the next job to materialize. It came with a call to arms in a subsidiary role as a legionary commander. The Social War (91–88 BC) was a protest by a confederacy of Italian states who were effectively tired of having to fight for Rome without being treated in the same way as Roman citizens, and of being deprived of participating in the decisions which required them to fight. The philosopher, historian, and biographer Plutarch (c. AD 46– c. 120), who wrote in Greek, suggests that Marius, at the age of 67, had somewhat lost his touch as a commander in the field. Certainly, when new military appointments were subsequently being handed out, he was conspicuously ignored. In particular, command of the army in the east in 88 BC against Mithridates, king of Pontus, who had invaded the Roman province of Asia and massacred the entire Roman and Italian business community, 80,000 men and their families, was given by the senate to Sulla, who was consul for that year.

The Italian states lost the Social War, but won their point. Full Roman citizenship was now effectively conceded to all peoples south of the river Po, with devolved local governments. Voting rights at the centre of power in Rome were still restricted, however, in that the newly enfranchised were not distributed equally among the 35 tribes.

15

Marius, who strongly resented being passed over for the eastern command, which he regarded as his by seniority and experience, now threw in his lot with Sulpicius Rufus, a tribune of considerable political ability and an arresting public speaker. Sulpicius's proposed legislation included a more equitable distribution among the tribes of the newly enfranchised Italians, and also of freedmen, the expulsion from the senate of all members owing more than 8000 sesterces (which would please equestrians to whom it was due), and the recall of exiles. It also called for the transfer of the eastern command from Sulla to Marius.

The senate responded by ordering a general suspension of public business, which was clearly unconstitutional. Sulpicius mobilized a band of armed supporters. There were violent clashes in the forum, in which the son of Sulla's colleague in office, Quintus Pompeius Rufus, was killed, and Sulla himself was forced to take refuge in a nearby house, which turned out to be Marius's. The consuls now had no choice but to cancel the suspension of business, and Sulpicius's measures became law. Sulla went off in high dudgeon to join his legions, who had been mustering at Capua before embarking for the east. He was still consul, but he held on to his military command only by virtue of his troops' personal loyalty to him.

There followed a series of events of the most profound significance for the republic.

Sulla and his six legions marched on Rome. This was the first occasion on which Roman troops had been employed against Rome itself, and the first civil war in the city's history. The supporters of Marius and Sulpicius's faction, without regular troops of their own, capitulated. Sulla used his authority as consul to neutralize the powers of the tribunes of the people, and strengthen those of the senate. Sulpicius's laws were declared invalid as having been passed by force, and he himself was hunted down and killed. Marius was declared an outlaw, whom anyone was encouraged to kill with impunity.

Sulla then left for the east with his legions. He carried out his assignment with some distinction, but it occupied him for the next five years.

In the meantime Marius had escaped from the city with his life, pursued by Sulla's agents. He ended up in Africa, in the course of a series of adventures that might have been invented by John Buchan at his most improbable. Trying to avoid a troop of horsemen, he swam out to sea, supported by two slaves because of his bulk, to reach a passing ship, only to be put ashore again. He hid in forests, and then in marshes, from which he was dragged and escorted to the nearest town, naked and covered in slime. The town council decided that he must die. When none of the local citizens could be found willing to kill him, they sent a Gallic warrior to do the job while he was asleep. Marius woke, and challenged the man, who fled, shouting that he could not kill Gaius Marius. The councillors then had Marius hustled on board a ship, in which he reached Carthage. The Roman governor of the province of Africa sent a personal envoy to urge him to move on. When asked what he had to say, Marius 'sighed deeply and answered: "Go tell your master that you have seen Gaius Marius, a fugitive, sitting in the rubble of Carthage" ' (Plutarch, *Marius* 40).

Marius was hastened across the frontier into Numidia, where his adopted son (also called Gaius Marius) and a group of Marius's supporters had taken refuge. The king of Numidia, uncertain what to do with his unwanted guests, nevertheless refused to let them go. The younger Marius escaped with the help of one of the king's concubines, who had fallen for him. Father and son met on the shore, and had just got away in a fishing boat when the king's horsemen hove in sight, bent on recapturing them.

In Rome, Lucius Cornelius Cinna, one of the consuls for 87 BC, announced that he would reintroduce Sulpicius's measure to extend the franchise. There were violent clashes in the forum, and Cinna's consular colleague, Gnaeus Octavius, had him ejected from the city. Cinna won over the legion Sulla had left on guard duties in Campania, and then did the rounds of the Italian towns in the south, collecting more troops to bolster his motley force. Meanwhile, Marius had landed in Etruria with his fellow-exiles and 500 armed slaves. From the towns of Etruria he raised 6000 volunteers, with whom he captured and plundered Ostia. The two irregular armies joined up and blockaded the city of Rome. Many within it, on restricted rations, died of plague, which also infected the besieging armies.

The senate, which had elected Lucius Merula, the *flamen dialis* (priest of Jupiter, the senior of the priests dedicated to particular deities), to replace the absent Cinna as consul, now revoked the appointment and sent envoys to Cinna, who received them sitting in the curule chair on a raised platform. When asked to swear that there would be no bloodshed, Cinna refused to take any oath, but gave his promise that he would not willingly be responsible for anyone's death. Marius, standing behind the consular seat of office, remained silent during this exchange; clearly he did not regard himself as a party to any such agreement.

The gates of the city were opened, and the killing began. It went on for five days and nights, until even Cinna tired of slaughter. Gnaeus Octavius was killed where he sat, in his chair of office and wearing his consular robes. Then his head was cut off and brought to Cinna, who had it hung up in the forum, where it was joined by those of a number of senators. This was the first time that the citizens of Rome had been presented with such a spectacle. It was by no means the last.

Slaves as well as soldiers went on the rampage. All Sulla's friends were murdered. His house was razed to the ground, his belongings were confiscated, and he himself was declared an enemy of the state. His wife and children would have been killed too, had they not managed to escape. Marius's appetite for vengeance was insatiable. Not even his friends were safe. If anyone greeted him in the street, and got no nod of recognition in return, it was the signal for Marius's bodyguard to kill them.

Under the guise of legality, false charges were laid against other prominent citizens. These included the blameless Merula, who, rather than face the ghastly charade of a trial, opened his veins on the very altars of the temple of Jupiter, having first carefully removed his sacred cap of office. Then Marius and Cinna declared themselves consuls for the succeeding year of 86 BC. It was Marius's seventh term of office, but he served only 17 days of it. According to Plutarch, he died of drink and delirium, and all Rome rejoiced at his death.

Julius Caesar was 13 at the time. He was born in Rome and his home was there throughout his life. Whether or not he was actually in the city during the grim siege and its even grimmer aftermath, he had good reason to recall them. For Julia, wife of Gaius Marius, was his aunt.

SULLA

# 2

# THE MAN IN THE MAKING
# 100–73 BC

He is said to have been tall, pale-complexioned, with a fine figure, rather full lips, and piercing black eyes. His health was good, though latterly he was liable suddenly to faint and also to suffer from nightmares. Twice he had an epileptic fit during a military campaign. He was rather fastidious about his appearance. He had himself shaved often, and what hair there was on his head was regularly trimmed. It was rumoured that he had depilatory treatment elsewhere on his body, too. He was acutely embarrassed by his baldness, which was a frequent subject of jokes on the part of his opponents. He took to combing his straggling locks forward from the back, and of all the honours heaped on him by senate and people, the one he appreciated best and took advantage of most often was the privilege of wearing a laurel wreath at all times. He also dressed in an unusual fashion. Instead of the short-sleeved, unbelted tunic which senators wore, his had long sleeves with a fringe at the wrists, and a belt fastened loosely round his waist; whence Sulla's frequent warning to the *optimates*, 'Beware of the improperly dressed boy!'

Suetonius, *Julius Caesar* 45

19

Gaius Julius Caesar, the balding dandy who is the subject of this near-contemporary report, was born in Rome on 13 July 100 BC or, according to some modern authorities, 102 BC. After his death, his official birthday was publicly celebrated on 12 July, since the 13th clashed with the games dedicated to Apollo, on which an oracle had declared that no other festivities in honour of a god should be held. The three names a Roman boy was given at birth comprised his personal *praenomen* (first name), the *nomen* (name) of his *gens* (clan), and his *cognomen* (family name). The Julii were patricians whose eminence was rooted in the mythological origins of Rome, rather than in practical achievement. His paternal grandfather was married to Marcia, who claimed to be descended from Ancus Marcius, fourth historical king of Rome. They had three children, of whom Julia married Marius, and Gaius Julius Caesar senior struggled up the ladder to become praetor in 91 BC, having earlier served as a member of one of Saturninus's land commissions.

Gaius Julius married Aurelia, four of whose family had achieved the consulate, the latest being her father, Lucius Aurelius Cotta, the consul in 119 BC who was threatened by Marius in the senate. They had, as far as is known, three children, Gaius Julius Caesar, Julia (major), and Julia (minor), whose grandson became the emperor Augustus. Girls were usually restricted to a feminine variation of the clan name, sometimes with the addition of a form of their father's *cognomen*.

If Caesar's earliest biographers, Plutarch and Suetonius (*c.* AD 70–*c.* 130), had anything to say about his childhood and upbringing, it is lost. We do know, from a throwaway remark in a speech in the senate made about him in 56 BC, that close early companions in Rome were Marcus Tullius Cicero and his brother Quintus (respectively six and four years older than Caesar), and their cousin, Gaius Varro. The Ciceros came from Arpinum, and had a house in Rome. It is not difficult to surmise that the connection between the two families was Marius.

Suetonius does record, however, that Caesar's juvenile literary works included a poem, 'In Praise of Hercules', a tragedy, 'Oedipus', and a book called 'Collected Sayings'. We do not know whether the last was compiled from Caesar's own dicta, or from those of others. If the former, then it would suggest a young man with an inbred self-confidence and an assurance of his destiny, though, as it transpired, he had to graft hard to achieve his ambitions; if the latter, then it illustrates his breadth of reading at an early age or an acquaintance, through his father and his uncle Marius, with prominent conversationalists or simply men of power and influence.

Education, from infancy to early manhood, was a sine qua non in upper-class Roman families. Basic literacy and numeracy were wide spread, even among slaves whose functions were purely manual. Originally, education had been exercised from within the family. A boy learned practical and martial arts from his father, who as head of the family had complete control over his

*Figure 2.1* A family group, from the *Ara Pacis*. The Latin word *familia*, from which the English word 'family' derives, had the meaning of 'household', including the property itself and all who lived in it. (C. M. Dixon/Ancient Art & Architecture Collection)

household, even on matters of life and death. Mothers taught their daughters moral precepts as well as domestic crafts.

Latterly during the republic, there developed a system of formal education under the influence of Greece. Greek-speaking slaves poured through the slave-markets of the Mediterranean, from Macedonia, Thrace, and the Greek mainland, and also from the eastern regions of the empire and the lands beyond, which had been Hellenized by the Macedonian king, Alexander the Great, in his lightning campaigns in 334–323 BC. Not only was the Latin alphabet derived from the Greek, but the Latin language, originally used only in the area of Latium, had been considerably enriched by features of Greek. Alongside the Latin writing masters, who were mainly freedmen or slaves, there grew up a class of *grammatici*, who taught Greek, initially as a means simply of practical communication which would have been essential for anyone indulging in trade. Latin literature had been slow to take off; its serious beginnings can be traced to the efforts of a former slave, Livius Andronicus, who in about 250 BC translated Homer's *Odyssey* into Latin. Just as without a close acquaintance with Latin literature on the part of writers in other languages, there would have been little English or European literature before the eighteenth century AD, so Latin literature itself derived largely from Greek models. Later historians of Rome, Appian (early second century

AD) and Cassius Dio (*c.* AD 164–*c.* 235), and also Plutarch, wrote in Greek because that was their first language. The earliest historians of Rome, Fabius Pictor and Cincius Alimentus, both members of the senate towards the end of the third century BC, wrote in Greek for literary reasons; it probably did not occur to them to write in Latin.

The typical Roman primary, or elementary, single-teacher school operated in shop premises, open to the street. It was probably attended by girls as well as boys, who would be conducted from and to home by a *paedagogus* (Greek for a slave-attendant), who was also responsible for his charges' manners and morals. At the age of about 12, boys went on to grammar school, followed at about 15 by training in rhetoric (the art of public speaking) and Greek philosophy. At all three levels, teaching was by Greek methods.

Those who could afford to do so, and were sufficiently inclined, employed a home tutor for their children. Such a teacher was Marcus Antonius Gnipho, from the Italian province of Cisalpine Gaul (Gaul this side of the Alps). His parents had exposed him at birth, a practice that was legal under the republic and for some time later. He was brought up as a slave, but freed by his owner and sent to be educated in Alexandria, then the capital city of Egypt and alternative centre of Greek learning. His first job after his return to Italy was to teach the young Caesar in the latter's home. Subsequently, he gave instruction in his own home, to men of distinction as well as to the young. Though he died before he was 50, he became so eminent in his field that he had no fixed fees, but left it to his pupils to decide how much they had benefited from his teaching. In that way, it is said that he earned much more than he otherwise would have done.

It was from Gnipho, then, that the young Caesar imbibed Greek as well as Latin language and literature, and the principles of oratory. Philosophy and advanced rhetoric would come later. It is fair to conclude that, like other Roman intellectuals of his time such as Cicero, Caesar read and spoke Greek as fluently as Latin, and probably was able to think in Greek as well – certainly, at significant moments in his career he was as likely to quote Greek as Latin. It may also be that he conversed in Greek with the most spectacular of his numerous mistresses, Cleopatra, queen of Egypt, whose first language was Greek.

In some quarters, however, the new-fangled Greek learning, and especially Greek philosophy, were frowned upon. Cicero's paternal grandfather observed, 'Our young men are like Syrian slaves; those who best know Greek are the most worthless' (Cicero, *On Oratory* II. 66. 265). It was a conflict of national ideals as well as of cultures. Though Athenians (among whom the culture of classical Greece began) and Romans both aimed to train their youth to serve the state, the ancient Greeks, with their traditions of music as well as of literature, concentrated on the intellectual being. By the time the full force of Greek influence began to be felt by Rome, the golden age of Greek culture had passed, and the Romans did not yet have anything of their own with which to replace it. Further, the Roman religion of the state, reflected also in the religion of the home and worship in the fields, with their reliance on ritual and superstition, had no place for philosophical or intellectual insights. Roman intellectuals, women as well as men, were turning to philosophy, exercised by Greeks, for guidance and consolation. In the eyes of the traditionalists, such people were undermining the religion of the state, and thus the state itself.

Greek ideas on physical training, too, differed from those of the Romans. To the Greeks, its object was largely to match the physical with the intellectual, to develop ease and grace of movement as well as of mind. Athletes who excelled in the great national games received the highest honours. To the Romans, though ball games, spear and quoit throwing, swimming and riding, and other energetic bodily pursuits were part of the daily routine, these were regarded as mere amusements, or were undertaken to make men fitter for active service. In particular, the Greek penchant for performing gymnastics, running, and wrestling in the nude went against Roman notions of decorum. To the Romans of Caesar's time, to resort to the gymnasium, as Greek youths consistently did, was a sign of immorality as well as of idleness.

In Caesar himself, physical and intellectual abilities were both developed to high degrees. These stood him in good stead when, almost by accident, he became a professional soldier, and found that the occupation suited his temperament and skills. He was a magnificent swordsman and horseman who would ride at full gallop with his hands behind his back – and without stirrups, which were not in use at this time. He was also a fine swimmer, an attribute that saved his life in Alexandria in 48 BC. His physical and mental energies, whether innate or acquired by training of body and mind, were inexhaustible.

On the death of Marius in Rome in 86 BC, Cinna had appointed Lucius Valerius Flaccus as his consular colleague; at the end of the year, he coolly nominated himself and Gnaeus Papirius Carbo consuls for the next two years. Carbo had, as a radical tribune of the people, proved himself a capable politician; he was also an able barrister. The intention of Cinna's policy of extended rule was likely to have been to ensure some continuous stability of government during the aftermath of unprecedented violence, at a time when the potential threat loomed of a return of Sulla from the east.

For what happened now to Caesar, we have only the testimony of Suetonius:

> [Julius Caesar] lost his father when he was 15. In the course of
> the next consulate [i.e. 84 BC], having been named *flamen dialis*, he
> broke off his betrothal, arranged when he was a boy, to Cossutia,
> whose family were equestrians, but extremely wealthy, and married

Cornelia, the daughter of four-times consul Cinna. Subsequently
they had a daughter, Julia.

Suetonius, *Julius Caesar* 1

It would appear that in common with other potentially great men such as the
Gracchi and Augustus, Caesar's education and upbringing had been directed
by his mother, who no doubt went on performing that function, insofar as it
was required, after her husband's death. Certainly she continued to live with
Caesar, even after his second marriage.

The rest of Suetonius's brief account of events of the year 84 BC requires
some explanation. The post of *flamen dialis* was so hedged around with
unusual taboos, as well as hazards, that its incumbent, let alone a teenage
incumbent, could hardly lead a normal life. The second-century AD antiquar-
ian Aulus Gellius wrote while he was in Greece a miscellany of essays, *Attic
Nights*, for the amusement and instruction of his children, in which he
described these restrictions. Among those that he could remember were that
the *flamen dialis* may not ride a horse, see an armed military force outside the
sacred boundary of the city of Rome, or walk under vines that were sprouting
upwards. He must not touch or even mention a nanny-goat, uncooked meat,
ivy, or beans, or come into contact with flour containing yeast. Only a free
man may cut his hair. If a person is brought into his house in fetters, he must
be untied and the bonds pulled out through the open skylight onto the roof
and then let down into the street. He must wear his pointy white cap of
office at all times – not until the first century AD was he allowed to dispense
with it indoors. He must not enter any place in which there is a tomb, or
touch a corpse, though he may take part in a funeral procession. The feet of
his bed are to be spread with a thin covering of clay. He may not sleep
elsewhere for three nights running, and it is forbidden for anyone to share his
bed. Similar, but less restrictive, prohibitions were laid on his wife, but if she
predeceased her husband, he had to resign his post.

It must have been due to the Marius connection that a mere boy was
selected as Merula's successor for this extraordinary, but highly prestigious,
office: so prestigious that not only the high priest himself, but also his wife,
must be of a patrician family. Cossutia came from a line of architects,
sculptors, and dealers in marble, but it was probably her wealth that first
attracted the Julii, who, if they had means at all, may have had them
invested in property and would have had need of ready cash. For the first but
by no means the last time in his life, Caesar made a politically-motivated
personal decision, or on this occasion had it made for him. Cossutia was
unceremoniously dumped, and he married Cinna's daughter Cornelia. Caesar
was over the minimum age of 14 for marriage of a male. If the main object
of the match with the Cossutii was money, then it must be assumed that
the marriage had not yet taken place because Cossutia was still under the
minimum age of 12 for a bride.

24

Suetonius implies that Caesar never actually took up the post of *flamen dialis*. Boys donned the *toga virilis*, signifying manhood, during their sixteenth year, which Caesar had already reached. He was also, by virtue of his father's death, *paterfamilias*, head of his family. It might still be argued that the office was being kept warm for him until he was regarded as old enough formally to assume its trappings and responsibilities, and that he was prevented from doing this by subsequent events. The Roman historians Tacitus (AD 56/7–*c.* 117) and Cassius Dio, however, state categorically that the post was not filled after the death of Merula until 11 BC, though the ceremonies associated with Jupiter continued uninterrupted. It has therefore been suggested that by opening his veins over the altars of Jupiter, Merula had polluted the temple to such an extent that before a new *flamen dialis* could take office, the sacred precinct had to be fully reconsecrated and a lengthy sequence of vows fulfilled. The process was delayed because in 83 BC the temple of Jupiter was destroyed by fire. Its replacement was not finished until 46 BC, and, having been several times damaged by lightning, was eventually restored at great expense by Augustus. It was he, too, who re-established the office of *flamen dialis*.

The year 84 BC was also that in which Caesar, *flamen dialis* elect, and just married, lost his father-in-law. Sulla's campaigns against Mithridates were showing signs of successful conclusion. Cinna, in order to avert civil war in Italy when Sulla returned, determined to face Sulla's army in Greece on its way back to Rome, but was murdered by his own troops at Ancona, while arranging their embarkation. Carbo soldiered on as sole consul until the end of the year, while Rome waited for the next political crisis.

It began in the spring of 83 BC, when Sulla landed unopposed at Brundisium with 40,000 troops. He was joined from different parts of the empire by three young men in particular to whom the Marian regime was repugnant and who felt that the future of Rome lay in Sulla's hands. From Africa came Quintus Caecilius Metellus Pius, son of Quintus Metellus Numidicus. The Latin word *pietas*, from which comes the adjective *pius*, can only be accurately translated as a combination of duty, devotion, and loyalty, to the gods and to one's relations and country. Quintus Metellus Pius had earned his surname by his efforts to arrange the recall of his father from exile. After the death of Cinna, he enlisted a private army in Africa, but had been defeated by the Roman governor of the province.

Marcus Licinius Crassus arrived from Spain, to which he had escaped after Cinna secured power in Rome. His father, Publius Licinius Crassus, who had been in the defence force of Rome against Marius and Cinna, had committed suicide when they took the city.

And then there was Pompey. Gnaeus Pompeius was the son of Gnaeus Pompeius Strabo, a professional soldier who had served as sole consul in 89 BC after his colleague was killed in the Social War. When Strabo's term of office was over, he retained the personal army he had raised mainly from his estates

*Figure 2.2* Silver *denarius* (= 4 sesterces) of about 54 BC showing the heads of the consuls for 88 BC, Sulla (obverse) and Quintus Pompeius Rufus (reverse), coined in their memory by the moneyer Quintus Pompeius Rufus, who was the grandson of both men. (× 2)

in Picenum. Sulla, as consul for 88 BC, seeing this as a threat to himself, arranged for the senate to order his consular colleague, Quintus Pompeius Rufus, to take over the command. Strabo, having appeared to acquiesce, then stood by while his troops lynched Rufus. When Marius and Cinna marched on Rome, Strabo and his troops put up a defence, but it was rumoured that he was also negotiating with Cinna. He died in the outbreak of plague in the city, so hated by the mob that they dragged his body through the streets on a hook.

Pompey was just 19 at the time. His house was looted by Cinna's hooligans, but he escaped injury or death, only then to be prosecuted for illegal possession of property acquired during the Social War, in which he fought under his father, as also did Cicero. Pompey was acquitted, thanks largely to his own forensic oratory and that of a defence team which included Carbo, but also no doubt to the fact that he was engaged to Antistia, the daughter of the president of the court, whom he later married as his first wife.

When the news reached Pompey that Sulla was preparing to return to Italy, he busied himself raising an illegal army in the vicinity of Picenum, where his family estates lay. Among those he recruited as officers were three men who were later to serve him well in their different ways: Lucius Afranius, Aulus Gabinius, and Titus Labienus. With a makeshift army which ultimately comprised about 18,000 men, the equivalent of three legions, he marched south to meet Sulla. On the way he defeated three separate armies of Carbo, who had retained his military *imperium* after his service as consul. Sulla meanwhile had seen off the armies of the consuls for 83 BC, Gaius Norbanus and Lucius Scipio. Norbanus he defeated by superior force of arms. He was going through the motions of negotiating with Scipio, when Scipio's troops deserted en masse and came over to Pompey's side. Scipio had, however, violated the temporary cessation of hostilities when his general, Quintus Sertorius, on his way to consult Norbanus about the terms, took possession of the town of Suessa, which supported Sulla.

When Pompey learned that he was now almost within hailing distance of Sulla, he ordered his troops to spruce themselves up and march to attention. When they met, the two victorious commanders, Pompey in his early twenties and Sulla in his late fifties, hailed each other as *imperator*. It was Pompey's first taste of public glory.

There was, however, still work to be done. The consuls for 82 BC were Carbo and young Marius, who at 27 was well under the legal age for the post, but had taken a leaf out of his father's book by arranging his own election, much, it is said, to the disapproval of his mother. At the head of one army, Marius tried to prevent Sulla getting to Rome by blocking the routes through Latium, but was himself besieged in Praeneste. The neighbouring Samnites, whose leaders Sulla had executed for refusing to disarm after the Social War, came out in support of Marius. There was fierce fighting beneath the very walls of Rome, just outside its north-eastern gate. Sulla, on the left wing of his army, was in desperate straits, but Crassus, commanding the right, wrapped up the battle by destroying or putting to flight all the Samnite opposition that he could see. The troops in Praeneste surrendered. Marius killed himself. According to Appian (*Civil Wars* I. 94), his head was sent to Rome, where it was mounted on a spike, while Sulla quoted a line from the Greek: ' "Learn first to row, before you take the helm" ' (Aristophanes, *Knights* 542).

Meanwhile, Carbo had abandoned the other consular army in the north and fled to Africa. Pompey, serving under Metellus who, as a former praetor, outranked him, mopped up the remnants of his troops.

Caesar was 18 when Sulla entered Rome in triumph. He had displayed his political instinct by giving no overt support to the constitutional movement led by his first cousin, Marius, and by Carbo. As nephew, however, of the elder Marius and son-in-law of Cinna, his position was precarious.

When Pompey returned to Rome, Sulla had a pleasant surprise for him. He would ally Pompey to his family and also to the Metelli, by giving him in marriage his stepdaughter Aemilia, whose mother, Sulla's wife, was the daughter of Metellus Delmaticus, consul in 119 BC, and whose father, Marcus Aemilius Scaurus, had been consul in 115 BC. This was a glittering match. Pompey divorced Antistia. A divorce between a very pregnant Aemilia and her husband was discreetly arranged, and the marriage took place. Pompey himself became a stepfather, but in this instance not a father, for a short time into the marriage Aemilia died as a result of a miscarriage. His third wife, Mucia, was the daughter of Mucius Scaevola, consul in 133 BC, and half-sister of two future consuls from the Metellus clan, Quintus Metellus Celer and Quintus Metellus Nepos. They had several children, including Gnaeus Pompeius and Sextus Pompeius. Like Caesar, Pompey was one of Rome's most eligible husbands. Each of his five marriages had political overtones.

Sulla was an autocrat in the same mould as Marius, but he was a more astute politician. When he had entered Rome in November 82 BC, he was determined that, after liquidating his enemies, he would set about reorganizing the government by quasi-constitutional, if not strictly constitutional, means. The senate played into his hands by legalizing all his consular and post-consular acts, granting him a triumph for his victories in the east, and authorizing an equestrian statue of him to be erected prominently in the forum. The inscription on the statue would name him as *imperator*, and also as *felix* (blessed by fortune), which he adopted as a surname. Since one of the consuls was dead and the other absent without leave, and shortly to be dead, the senate, following the constitution, appointed its leader, Lucius Valerius Flaccus, as *interrex* (the equivalent under the republic of temporary head of government), one of whose responsibilities was to appoint *consules suffecti* (substitute consuls) to serve out the term of elected consuls who were unable to continue in office.

Sulla, however, would have none of this pussy-footing. By some means he persuaded Flaccus to propose to the *comitia centuriata* that he, Sulla, be appointed not consul but permanent dictator, with a brief to institute legislation and reconstitute the republic. This having been approved, he allowed the consular elections for 81 BC to go ahead, before getting down to business:

> He himself called the Roman people to assemble, and harangued them with an outburst of self-aggrandisement, mixed with menaces intended to put fear into them. He concluded by assuring his audience that he would lead the people to an existence which would be changed for the better, if they would comply with his wishes; not one of those opposed to him would be spared the ultimate punishment. He would prosecute vengeance of the utmost severity on praetors, quaestors, military tribunes, and anyone else who had acted in a hostile manner from the day on which Scipio had violated the peace agreement. He then pronounced sentence of death on forty senators and some 1600 equestrians. He seems to have been the first to proscribe those whom he wished murdered, to reward their executioners and those who informed on them, and to punish any found hiding the victims. Soon afterwards he added other senators to the list. Some of them, caught unawares, were killed where they were discovered, at home, in the street, in the temple. Some were bodily heaved up from where they were and thrown at Sulla's feet. Others were dragged through the streets and kicked to death, eye-witnesses being too frightened to utter a word of protest at the horrors they saw. Others were expelled from Rome or had their property and belongings confiscated. Spies were everywhere, looking for those who had fled the city.
>
> Appian, *Civil Wars* I. 11

The killing spread through Italy, as Sulla took revenge on regions which had opposed him. There was method, however, behind this particular outburst of calculated butchery. He needed land for his army veterans and for troops who were being stood down. For these he established colonies where he had devastated the countryside.

Nominally, the proscriptions were brought to a halt on 1 June 81 BC. Unofficially, they continued. During the late summer or autumn of that year, Sextus Roscius, a wealthy farmer from Ameria, a hill-town north of Rome, who had not been on the list, was murdered by thugs while walking back from a dinner party in Rome. Chrysogonus, one of Sulla's favoured freedmen, had Roscius's name added to the proscription list retrospectively in order to get his hands on Roscius's extensive property. As a result, when it had been formally confiscated and put up for auction, he secured it for one three-thousandth of its true value. In the face of justified complaints from outraged worthies of Ameria, Chrysogonus and two fellow conspirators from the town shifted the focus away from themselves by having Roscius's son, also called Sextus Roscius, accused of his father's murder, though he was at home in Ameria at the time.

Parricide was one of the most heinous crimes in Roman law. The penalty was to be flogged, and then sewn up in a sack with a dog, a cock, and a viper, and thrown into the sea or a river. Counsel for the defence was Cicero, at 26 just beginning his career as a barrister. In the light of Chrysogonus's relationship with Sulla, it was a courageous case to take on; it was even more courageous to insinuate to the court that the true villain of the piece was Chrysogonus. Roscius was resoundingly acquitted, and Cicero's forensic and political careers took off from that point. The case is also significant for his incorporating in his speech for the defence the first recorded reference to the legal maxim *cui bono* (who stood to gain?).

Sulla's constitutional reforms, properly voted through the *comitia centuriata*, included a wide range of measures designed to shore up a decaying republic by effectively, in the short term, restoring power to the upper classes. Civil wars, murders, and deaths by more natural causes had reduced the senate to about half its previous number of members, thus severely, and irrevocably, weakening the traditional republican element represented by the old aristocracy. Sulla doubled its original size by admitting some 300 equestrians and also Italian office holders from the regions outside Rome. While many of the new senators would naturally have been supporters of Sulla, he ensured its long-term future as a quasi-independent body by raising the number of quaestors, who were nominally elected by the people, from 12 to 20, and giving ex-quaestors automatic entry to the senate. He reapplied the statutory 10-year gap between holding the same office, and affirmed that the minimum ages for quaestors, aediles, praetors, and consuls should be adhered to. He increased from six to eight the number of praetors, with the result that after their terms of office there were, with the two ex-consuls, 10 new officials available to serve as provincial governors. He introduced measures which placed provincial governors, who by virtue of their office automatically had military as well as administrative *imperium*, under greater senatorial control. He sought to increase the authority of the senate by reducing the powers of the tribunes of the people, though these measures were repealed in 70 BC, when Crassus and Pompey were the consuls. Sulla also restored to the senate the exclusive right to sit on juries in the new courts he established to try major crimes, and he clarified the distinction between criminal and civil law.

Though still dictator, he offered himself as consul for 80 BC, with Metellus Pius as his consular colleague; they were duly elected. Pompey, at 24, was too young for political advancement. Sulla needed, however, his proven military skills, and despatched him to Sicily, whose Roman governor, Marcus Perperna Veiento, had declared himself to be in opposition to Sulla, and had been joined from Africa by Carbo. In order that Pompey might be seen to act in an official capacity, Sulla enjoined the senate to grant him an honorary *imperium*. Perperna fled without a fight, leaving Sicily in the hands of Pompey, whose men caught up with Carbo on the neighbouring island of Cossyra. The three-times consul was brought before young Pompey in chains, and then taken away to be executed.

Pompey was now posted to Africa, where in quick time he first defeated (and probably executed) Gnaeus Domitius Ahenobarbus, Cinna's son-in-law, who had established himself as governor; then he restored the rightful king of Numidia to his throne. Pompey's whole army now acclaimed him not only *imperator* but also *magnus* (great), which he subsequently adopted as a surname.

Meanwhile in Rome, Caesar had been in deep trouble. Sulla had taken advantage of the informal marriage procedures of the times to give Pompey an advancement in society. They had also been used to cement political affiliations when Marcus Pupius Piso, a former fellow law student of Cicero and quaestor in 83 BC, opted for Sulla's party and divorced his wife Annia, Cinna's widow, shortly after their marriage. Likewise, Marcus Aemilius Lepidus had divorced his wife, who was related to Saturninus, when he joined Sulla and profited from the proscriptions. Sulla now requested Caesar to divorce his wife Cornelia, Cinna's daughter. Caesar refused.

It is unlikely, but feasible, that Sulla had in mind for Caesar the kind of advantageous match with which he briefly blessed Pompey. It is more probable that Sulla was simply carrying out a policy of disarming those who might oppose him politically for reasons of family loyalty. It is not known for certain when Caesar and Cornelia's daughter Julia was born, but the consensus of scholarship is now that it was not until about 76 BC; in which case, that was not a factor in Caesar's decision. Marriage by *confarreatio*, a ritual involving a sacred loaf which was compulsory for senior priests and which would have been employed at the wedding of Caesar and Cornelia, was at this time indissoluble. It may be that Caesar gave this justification for refusing to divorce Cornelia. Or it may be simply that he loved her.

Sulla was not a man to take no for an answer. According to Suetonius, he responded by sacking Caesar from his position as *flamen dialis* elect, confiscating both his inheritance from his father and his wife's dowry, and treating him as a political enemy. Caesar went into hiding from Sulla's secret agents. He changed his place of refuge almost every day, using the houses of friends where he could, or else bribing the householders. All this time he was suffering from a bout of malaria, a persistent health hazard in Rome, where the mosquitoes bred in the swampy ground at the foot of the hills, in the sewers, and in the streets themselves.

Caesar, however, still had friends in very high places, or Sulla had a streak of humanity which is not evident elsewhere. Among those who interceded with Sulla on Caesar's behalf were his cousin on his mother's side, Gaius Aurelius Cotta, consul in 75 BC, and the vestal virgins, high-born members of that exclusive branch of the pontifical college, the senior religious body of the state. Not only did they intercede, they went on interceding until Sulla grudgingly yielded: ' "I give up! You can have him! But remember that the man you are so keen to save will one day destroy the cause of the ruling party which you and I are trying to uphold. There are many signs of Marius in Caesar" ' (Suetonius, *Julius Caesar* 1).

Caesar's position in Rome was still untenable. He was 18, and he had no job. One was found for him abroad, as a military attaché on the staff of Marcus Thermus, the governor of the Roman province of Asia. It was a plum posting for a young man with ambitions, because though Sulla had engineered a peace treaty in the east, hostilities between Rome and Mithridates had never properly been brought to a halt. Thus there were opportunities for diplomacy, military action, and who knows what else. Caesar managed to enjoy all three.

His initial assignment was to visit the court of Nicomedes IV, ruler of the Black Sea coastal kingdom of Bithynia, to organize and bring back a squadron of ships. Nicomedes was an ally of Rome, having been restored to his throne by Sulla after Mithridates had deposed him. The ships were needed by Thermus for an assault on Mytilene, the fortress capital of the island of Lesbos, which still held out for Mithridates. Caesar spent enough time at court for scandalous innuendos to be spread that he had prostituted himself to Nicomedes; these resurfaced when, having completed his mission, Caesar returned to Bithynia, ostensibly to pick up some money which was owed to one of his freedmen. In both Greek and Roman society, the penetration by a male of a younger man, or a man of inferior status, was regarded as perfectly normal, and Nicomedes may have taken especial pride in having bedded a handsome, young, aristocratic Roman. The same did not hold for the male who was being used: to be sexually penetrated was regarded as thoroughly shameful. Whatever did, or did not, happen, this episode returned to haunt

Caesar in later years, as such things tend to do, at the height of his military and political career.

Caesar took part in the actual storming of Mytilene, with conspicuous gallantry. Afterwards Thermus presented him with the *corona civica* (civic crown), a wreath of oak leaves awarded for saving a Roman life in battle. It was worn on festive occasions, and when a recipient made an appearance at the public games, the whole audience, including senators, rose from their seats.

Meanwhile in Rome in 79 BC, for which year the consuls were Publius Servilius Vatia and Appius Claudius Pulcher, son of the father-in-law of Tiberius Gracchus, there was a political sensation. Sulla had resigned! After three years of what was effectively a return to the monarchy, he gave up his dictatorship and all other public offices, and retired to his estate at Puteoli, to write his memoirs. What remained of his life was spent in riotous living and entertaining, and in a late second marriage to an attractive young divorcée called Valeria, whom he had spotted when she passed him at a gladiatorial show. His death in 78 BC was, however, undignified and painful. He had just, according to Plutarch, finished Book 22 of his autobiography, when he succumbed to a thoroughly nasty dose of phthiriasis (infestation of lice), which developed from an ulcerous condition. He was given a state funeral, organized by Pompey, who, however, had been cut out of Sulla's will because of his support for Marcus Aemilius Lepidus, who stood for consul on a *popularis* ticket and was elected for 78 BC, with Quintus Lutatius Catulus, a leader of the *optimates* and son of the consul of 102 BC, as his consular colleague.

Caesar was still in the east when Sulla died. He was now attached to the staff of Servilius Vatia, who after his term as consul had been appointed governor of Cilicia, with a special brief to take action against the pirates who operated from its coasts. With Sulla dead, Caesar was free to rejoin his family. With Sulla dead, he needed to know where he should line up in the inevitable political maelstrom.

Disagreement between the two consuls in 78 BC developed into open war between ex-consuls in 77 BC, when Marcus Lepidus got together a revolutionary army with which he marched on Rome, but was defeated by Catulus. The senate mobilized Pompey, again with a special *imperium* for which he did not qualify, to put down trouble in the north, where Marcus Junius Brutus, Marcus Lepidus's second-in-command, was raising troops. Pompey besieged Marcus Junius Brutus in Mutina and then, having accepted his surrender, had him assassinated. Marcus Lepidus took refuge in Sardinia, where, according to Plutarch, he became ill and died of remorse, not at his public humiliation, but at having discovered a letter to his wife written by her lover. Pompey meanwhile made no attempt to disband his troops, but waited for the next call. It came in the form of an assignment to help Metellus Pius, governor of Further Spain, against Quintus Sertorius, formerly Cinna's man, who had now rebelled against Rome. The war took Pompey until 71 BC to bring to a satisfactory conclusion.

Though, according to Suetonius, Marcus Lepidus made overtures to Caesar, whose political sympathies lay with the *populares*, and promised him military promotion, Caesar had turned him down: he did not have enough confidence in Marcus Lepidus's ability or in the prospects for political change at this time. Significantly, however, he does not seem to have made any attempt openly to oppose Marcus Lepidus's party, but instead threw himself into a completely different line of activity. The only careers open to young men of his social class were the army, the law, and politics. He was still too young to go into politics, so at the age of 23 he became a barrister: not in a junior capacity, but as a principal prosecutor. In this he could be said to be following in the footsteps of his father's first cousin, Gaius Julius Caesar Strabo Vopiscus, orator and wit, part of one of whose speeches Caesar borrowed in an early courtroom oration. According to Suetonius, Caesar spoke in a high voice, with extravagant gestures.

Caesar decided that it would be good for his image to act in the appropriate court for the people of Macedonia in their case for extortion against the former consul Gnaeus Cornelius Dolabella, who, they claimed, had unfairly enriched himself while governor of the province in 79 BC. Cornelius Dolabella was represented by two of the foremost members of the Roman bar, Gaius Aurelius Cotta, who as Caesar's cousin had pleaded for him with Sulla, and Quintus Hortensius Hortalus, an orator of legendary skill which he was not beneath reinforcing with bribery, chicanery, and intimidation. Caesar lost the case, but made his name. He published his speeches for a wider audience, including the Greeks who retained him to prosecute Gaius Antonius, a military associate of Sulla who had used his position to milk the province during the wars against Mithridates. He would have won his case, too, had not Gaius Antonius, in desperate straits, successfully appealed to the tribunes of the people to halt the trial.

The ease with which Caesar had mastered the craft of advocate belied his age, and was the subject of informed comment by historians and by the first-century AD rhetorician and critic, Quintilian:

> If, in fact, Caesar had had the time to practise at the bar, he alone could have been regarded as the equal of Cicero. He was so forceful, incisive, passionate, that it would appear he was as inspired a speaker as he was a general. His precision of language, of which he was an assiduous student, enhanced his mastery of the art.
>
> *Institutio Oratia* X. 114

Yet Caesar now went abroad again, ostensibly to improve his powers of oratory by studying in Rhodes under Apollonius Molon, a rhetorician whose lectures in Rome had impressed Cicero, who also took lessons from him. It has been suggested that Caesar's dignified exit from Rome at this time was to avoid the attentions of those who might take issue with his prosecution of supporters of the Sullan regime. There is an equally likely scenario: Sulla had established that the minimum legal age for election to quaestor was 30, and Caesar was still only 25. It is probable that Caesar already had his eye on a political career. The poet Lucan (AD 39–65) described him as 'obsessed by action, and thought he had done nothing while anything was left to do' (*The Civil War* II. 656–7). Caesar had proved himself in the courts. He could not bear to sweat it out in Rome for five years, at a time when the volatile political situation might necessitate his taking sides before he was ready to play a positive role.

If he was looking for action, however, action soon overtook him. On the way to Rhodes, following the coast of the province of Asia, his ship was captured by pirates off the island of Pharmacusa. They demanded a ransom of 20 talents of silver for his release – a Greek talent weighed 26.24 kilos. Caesar protested that he was worth far more than that, and instructed his crew to go around the neighbouring towns and raise 50 talents, while he remained hostage, attended by his doctor and two valets. The pirates, from Cilicia, were a bloodthirsty lot, but this did not disconcert him in the slightest. He joined in their sports and physical exercises, and practised his public speaking on them. He promised any hecklers that he would in due course string them up. The pirates took this as a great joke.

When, after a month, the ransom money arrived, Caesar paid it over, obtained his freedom, and sailed for the nearby port of Miletus. There he hired a squadron of light ships and returned to Pharmacusa, where he found the pirate fleet still at anchor. He captured several of the ships, took their pirate crews prisoner, and relieved them of their booty. He then had the men secured in prison in Pergamum, the capital of the province, and asked Marcus Juncus, Thermus's successor, for instructions as to their punishment. When Juncus dithered, thinking he might make some money by ransoming the pirates, Caesar, on his own initiative, had them crucified, as he had undertaken to do. Being of a merciful disposition, however, he first had their throats cut. Then he continued his passage to Rhodes.

In late 75 or early 74 BC, Nicomedes died without an heir, bequeathing his kingdom to Rome. Mithridates reopened hostilities by sending a force into Bithynia, which commanded the entrance to the Black Sea, thinking that it would be easy to wrest the territory from its new owners. At the same time, he sent a southern column actually into the province of Asia itself. Caesar, again on his own initiative, crossed over to the mainland, raised a body of troops locally, and drove Mithridates's force back into its own territory. Then he resumed his studies in Rhodes.

There is some suggestion that following this demonstration of organizational and tactical skills, Caesar was later in 74 BC attached as a senior officer to the staff of Marcus Antonius (brother of Gaius Antonius and father of

Mark Antony), who, as praetor, had been assigned the task of dealing with the Mediterranean pirates. This being so, Caesar would have been stationed on the coast of Laconia, at the southern tip of Greece. He was not there long. In 73 BC he set off back to Rome, having learned that he had been appointed a priest of the pontifical college, replacing his cousin, Gaius Aurelius Cotta, who had died. In order to avoid the attentions of pirates, he made the actual crossing of the Adriatic Sea, probably to Brundisium, in an open, four-oared boat, accompanied by two friends and ten slaves. On their way, he spotted on the horizon what looked like the masts and yards of a pirate fleet. He removed his outer garments, strapped a dagger to his thigh, and prepared to fight for his life, or to the death. Then he realized that what he had seen was a row of trees on the distant shore.

The 15 priests of the pontifical college, under their head, the *pontifex maximus*, were the leading administrators and organizers of the religion of the state, including sacrifices and the games, and the authorities on procedure and matters concerning the calendar and festivals, and the designation of particular days on which certain public business could not be conducted. All were of the nobility, some were themselves former consuls. To be one of their number carried considerable political prestige. Before he was old enough even to be a member of the senate, Caesar had impacted on the political scene. His energy, his all-round ability, his political instinct, and his luck ensured that he never left it.

CAESAR

# 3
# THE POLITICIAN 73–63 BC

The man who appears to me to be properly alive, and to enjoy
life, is engaged in something constructive, and seeks recognition by some famous deed or the exercise of a useful art. It is a
glorious thing to be of service to the state, nor is eloquence to
be despised. A man may achieve fame either in peacetime or in
war.

Sallust, *War of Catiline* 2–3

It was presumably as a holder of the *corona civica*, and in the light of his other
spectacular military performance, that Caesar was one of 24 elected in the
*comitia tributa* to serve as military tribunes for the year 72 BC. This process
was a throwback to pre-Marian times, when the six military tribunes in each
of the first four legions raised in any year were chosen by the people. After
about 200 BC, military tribunes ranked second to the legionary commander
(legate).

Whether or not Caesar actively participated in the events of 72 BC, it was a
momentous if also humiliating year in Roman military history. In 73 BC,
Spartacus, a Thracian slave, broke out of the gladiatorial training school at
Capua with a few companions. As the news spread, more and more slaves
from the rural areas joined him at his base on the then inactive Mount
Vesuvius. Three separate praetorian armies failed to dislodge them and had

to retire ignominiously. Spartacus wanted to withdraw across the Alps and seek freedom for his followers, who now numbered 70,000, but too many of them preferred to stay in Italy for the plunder; so reluctantly he wintered in the south. In 72 BC the senate woke up to the situation, and sent both consuls, with a legion each, against Spartacus, who despatched them singly and with their forces combined. Spartacus then determinedly marched north, defeating on the way the governor of Cisalpine Gaul, only to be persuaded to turn back once again. It was now even rumoured that he proposed to march on Rome.

At this point, enter Crassus. He had profited enormously from Sulla's proscriptions, but in the intervening years had had no further military experience. He had, however, been a praetor, and had enriched himself even more by discovering a niche in the property market. He built up a team of more than 500 slaves who specialized in architectural and building skills. At the first sign of fire in the city, a regular occurrence, he offered a nominal price not only for the burning building but for all the other houses in the neighbourhood. Under the circumstances the owners were only too pleased to accept. When the buildings had been refurbished by his team, he sold them at a vast profit or let them out at exorbitant rents. In this way, it was said that most of Rome belonged to him at one time or another.

Crassus now made the senate an offer which its members could hardly refuse. He would himself raise six legions, if the senate would grant him the *imperium* to lead them against Spartacus. The senate agreed. Many of those who joined Crassus were veterans of Sulla's campaigns. He stamped his authority on his troops right from the start, by reviving the punishment of decimation for 500 of his own men who had disobeyed orders. He divided them up into 50 groups of 10, and then had one man from each group publicly executed in front of the whole army.

In 71 BC Spartacus was in the toe of Italy, maybe with the intention of crossing to Sicily. He broke through the lines, 35 miles long, that Crassus had dug across the peninsula to hem him in, only for his army to be caught between Crassus's legions to the west and in the east those of Marcus Terentius Varro Lucullus, newly arrived at Brundisium after a successful military campaign as governor of Macedonia. Spartacus was killed. Crassus had 6000 of his followers crucified along the Appian Way from Capua to Rome.

Five thousand more escaped to the north and were mopped up by Pompey in Etruria. It is not clear whether he had been called back from Spain to help, or whether he just happened to be there at the conclusion of his campaign. Either way, he had the senate's backing, and he claimed that it was he, and not Crassus, who should take the credit for ending the slave insurrection. Crassus was not at all pleased, and, when anyone observed that Pompey the Great was coming, took to asking, ' "How big is great?" ' (Plutarch, *Crassus* 7).

The upshot, however, was that Crassus and Pompey, the latter six years younger than the minimum age for the post and never having held any public office, stood for election as consuls for 70 BC, and were returned unopposed. There was a further precedent. Pompey, anyway, was elected *in absentia*. The law stated that candidates for the consulship must present themselves in person in Rome. A victorious general, awarded a triumph, as Pompey was for his victories in Spain, must, however, remain outside the city limits until the day of the triumph if he was to retain his command. Pompey got his triumph by remaining with his troops. He also got the consulship. It was not always to be thus.

So, far from never having held public office, Pompey may never even have witnessed a meeting of the senate, except possibly as his father's guest when he was a boy, still less been aware of the procedures of a body over which he would be required to preside. He did, however, have a handbook on the subject, specially compiled for him by his friend Marcus Terentius Varro, scholar, politician, and writer. With the help of this, no doubt, and Crassus's experience, the two consuls for 70 BC initiated some constructive measures, including finally restoring to the tribunes their traditional powers, reforming the courts, and reviving the office of censor, which Sulla had abolished.

One of the measures which the new tribunate proposed was an amnesty for, and recall of, the former supporters of Marcus Lepidus and Sertorius. Caesar, who had an interest in the bill since one of those who would benefit by it was his brother-in-law Lucius Cinna, spoke eloquently on its behalf in a speech which he also published. We have another sight of him during this period, prosecuting Marcus Juncus in a court case for extortion, brought by the Bithynians. He claimed he was doing this out of respect for the hospitality he had received from Nicomedes, though doubtless there were also personal reasons for wishing to see Juncus in court.

In 69 BC, when, at the end of their term of office, Crassus returned to his business dealings and Pompey became a private citizen, Caesar began his political career in earnest. At the first possible opportunity under the rules laid down by Sulla, he had stood as candidate for a quaestorship and was elected. First, however, there was a family duty to perform. His aunt Julia, the widow of Marius, died, probably in her early sixties. It was customary for elderly women to be honoured with a eulogy at their funerals. Caesar turned the occasion into a political statement. He had wax images of Marius carried in the funeral procession, and then delivered from the *rostra*, the speakers' platform in the forum, a rousing address centring on Julia's royal and divine family origins:

> My aunt Julia was through her mother descended from the kings of
> Rome, and on her father's side she was related to the immortal gods.
> For the Marcii Reges [i.e. kings], the name of her mother's family,
> goes back to Ancus Martius, and the Julii, of whose clan we are a
> family, to the goddess Venus. Our line therefore is due the respect
> commanded by kings, who possess the greatest power among human

beings, and the worship owed to the gods, who hold even kings in their sway.

Suetonius, Julius Caesar 6

Very soon after this Caesar was giving a funeral oration for his wife. Cornelia was probably in her late twenties when she died, and it was unheard of for a young woman to be given a funeral eulogy. For Caesar it was an exercise in public relations, a demonstration to the people that he was a caring man. This done, he reported for duty as quaestor in Further Spain, leaving his six-year-old daughter Julia in the care of his mother.

As assistant to the provincial governor, his official function in Spain was to act as a peripatetic administrator of justice. Later, he claimed that he had 'given that province extra-special treatment, and had handed out as many benefits as were then in his power' (*Spanish War* 42. 2). Doubtless, not all the benefits were one way! Both Suetonius and Cassius Dio describe his coming across a statue of Alexander the Great in Cadiz: 'He gave a hearty sigh, as if disgusted at his own lack of direction in having done nothing at an age at which Alexander had already conquered the world' (Suetonius, *Julius Caesar* 7). The experience apparently so shattered him that he threw up his assignment before the governor had finished his term of office, and went home. On the way, he found himself caught up, or allowed himself to be caught up, in a demonstration of unrest among some of the Transpadane Gauls (Gallic peoples the far side of the river Po), who were demanding the same rights of citizenship as their neighbours south of that river. The *popularis* element in Caesar was sympathetic to their cause, but a potential uprising was scotched by the senate, who sent into the region two legions which had been held back from service in the east for just this eventuality.

Caesar's status as ex-quaestor automatically entitled him to a seat in the senate. He now married again. His second wife was Pompeia, granddaughter on her father's side of Sulla's consular colleague in 88 BC, and on her mother's side of Sulla himself. Presumably Caesar saw nothing inconsistent in marrying the granddaughter of the man who had sullied the name of his uncle-by-marriage, and been responsible for the death of his first cousin, as long as she had money. To be a successful politician involved continuous outflows of cash, in bribes for the electorate, public relations exercises in the form of ostentatious contributions to public works, and sweeteners in kind, such as public performances of the games. Caesar was also by nature wildly extravagant, to the extent that Plutarch estimated that before he ever held any office of state, he was in debt to the tune of 1300 talents – in terms of Roman coinage almost 35 million sesterces.

It was probably his new wife's contribution to the family finances that enabled him to catch the public eye by accepting in 67 BC the post of curator of the Appian Way, the main route from the south which ran from Brundisium to the capital. Since this was an *ad hoc* position, the inference is that the road had fallen into disrepair, and someone was required to organize the necessary work who could afford to subsidize it out of his own pocket, over and above what was available from the public treasury. His reward would be in the form of inscriptions on milestones advertising his contribution to the repairs, and plaudits from a grateful travelling public.

That same year, Aulus Gabinius used the powers that had been restored to the tribunes to propose in the *concilium plebis* the creation of the post of supreme military commander at sea and on land, with unlimited resources, to combat the Mediterranean pirates, whose predations had got completely out of hand. It was not so much the organized sacking and looting of 400 cities along the coasts and numerous sacred places of worship and refuge, the danger to ships and trade, and the disruption of the corn supply to Rome; it was the deliberate insolence displayed to Roman citizens. On one occasion they captured not one praetor, but two, in their official togas and with their attendants. On another they took hostage, and obtained a large ransom for, a sister of Marcus Antonius, who had been granted a wide *imperium* by the senate in 74 BC to get rid of them. Not only members of the Roman nobility were humiliated by the pirates: victims captured at sea who were not thought worth ransoming were treated to a grotesque charade. When a prisoner announced that he was a Roman citizen, the pirates pretended to be frightened out of their wits. They begged his pardon, found Roman boots for his feet, and dressed him in a toga, so that there would be no mistake next time. Then, when they had finished tormenting him, they sent him down a ship's ladder, rung by rung, into the sea. If he refused, they tossed him overboard to drown. The ordeal of 'walking the plank' is thus an ancient ritual.

It was a job for Pompey. Everyone knew that. Which was why the people gave their wholehearted support to the bill, and why the senate, almost down to a man, advised its rejection, fearing the consequences of one individual holding such military power over such a huge area, and possibly failing to relinquish it at the end of his mission. The exception in the senate was Caesar, who though only a junior member spoke in favour of the appointment.

The senate's advice was ignored, and the people's and Caesar's views prevailed: Pompey was handed the command and given three years in which to complete the assignment. He finished it in three months. The tribune Gaius Manilius now proposed a bill extending Pompey's command with the specific mandate of bringing to an end the wars against Mithridates, which had been bedevilling the Romans, and everyone else in the region, for over 20 years. Both Cicero, who was a praetor, and Caesar spoke in favour of the measure, and on this occasion the senate had no option but to give its blessing. Pompey succeeded brilliantly where his predecessors had failed, and in doing so considerably enlarged the empire and its revenue from taxes. He created new provinces, established city-states, and enrolled client-kingdoms.

He also vastly increased his personal following of clients, except among the Jews, whom he deeply offended by using excessive violence to settle their internecine affairs, and then forcing his way through the curtained sanctuary of the Temple into the Holy of Holies, which only the high priest was allowed to enter.

The restoration of tribunary powers had in these two instances worked to the benefit of the state, by giving unprecedented authority to one individual. It remained to be seen how the state would fare when they were employed less scrupulously.

Caesar, meanwhile, was continuing his way up the ladder of political advancement. He was elected for 65 BC one of the two curule aediles, who were responsible for orderly behaviour in the streets and markets of the city, and for the maintenance of temples and other public buildings. They were also obliged to subsidize out of their own pockets the games which were held on public holidays. Caesar's colleague in office was Marcus Bibulus, who contributed equal amounts, but somehow it was always Caesar who took the credit. Caesar also exploited the opportunity that his office offered to court the electorate by putting on, ostensibly at his own expense, additional performances of the games, as well as theatrical shows, processions, and public banquets. None of these was more extravagant than the games he mounted, somewhat belatedly, in honour of his father, who had died 20 years earlier. In these celebrations, 320 pairs of gladiators fought each other to the death, all in silver armour.

A further display of showmanship was designed to demonstrate his political alignments as well as flaunt his family connections. As dawn broke one day over the Capitol Hill, those who were out and about found themselves gazing at a splendid exhibition of Marius memorabilia and trophies, including exquisite golden artefacts looted during his wars against the Cimbri. Everyone knew who had arranged the display. In the course of an emergency debate in the senate, Lutatius Catulus, now acknowledged leader of the *optimates*, attacked Caesar in memorable terms: ' "You are no longer seeking to take over the state by undermining her, Caesar; you are now employing mechanical devices" ' (Plutarch, *Caesar* 6).

Where the money was now coming from would become public knowledge when Caesar was appointed to a provincial governorship in 61 BC. Having spent all his own financial resources, and probably his wife's, too, he was being bankrolled by Crassus, the richest man in Rome, whose avariciousness extended to moneylending on a vast scale. Crassus would buy in the debts of promising politicians, and hold them against the time when he would be repaid, with interest, from the profits to be made by a provincial governor. Caesar was now 35. He was ambitious for political advancement; it had also become an economic necessity. The regulations stipulated that he could not run for the office of praetor for another two years.

In 64 BC, Cicero was 42. He had been praetor in 66 BC, but he had waived his right to continued *imperium* and a provincial governorship in 65 BC, in order to make preparations to stand for the consulship for 63 BC, the elections for which would be held in June of the previous year. It was a fateful decision.

Not only was Cicero *novus homo*, who could not automatically count on the support of any grouping, but he did not have the resources to bribe the electorate. There were seven candidates in all, two of whom seemed to offer Cicero serious opposition: Gaius Antonius and Lucius Sergius Catilina (Catiline), both of whom were backed by Crassus. Cicero decided that his best chance lay in using his oratory and his forensic skills to discredit them. He had promising material with which to work.

Gaius Antonius, whom Caesar had prosecuted in 76 BC, was a thoroughly disreputable character who had been expelled from the senate in 70 BC, but had been allowed to resume his seat after being elected praetor for 66 BC. He was no leader, rather a man who would give his support to whoever led him, for better or for worse.

Catiline had tried to stand for election for 65 BC, after both the successful candidates had been disbarred for overenthusiastic bribery at the polls, but had been disqualified because he was awaiting trial for extortion during his tour of duty as governor of the province of Africa. Rumours surfaced later that he then conspired with the deposed consuls to assassinate the consuls who had replaced them, and that Caesar was somehow implicated. If there ever was such a plot, it is most improbable that Caesar was involved in it. He was a bender, not a breaker, of the law.

Catiline was also accused at various times of murder, including that of his own son, it was believed because the woman he wished to marry did not want a husband with grown-up offspring. He was also said to have had sex with a vestal virgin, and to have indulged in numerous other unspeakable profligacies.

In the end, Cicero was elected by an overwhelming majority, with Gaius Antonius as the other consul. Cicero promptly made a deal with his consular colleague. In return for being allowed to exercise complete control, he transferred to Gaius Antonius, in return for the promise of a small consideration, the governorship-elect of the province of Macedonia, with its prospect of rich pickings, which had been Cicero's privilege after his year of office. This suited Gaius Antonius down to the ground, and enabled Cicero to act as sole consul.

As the time approached for the elections for 62 BC, with Catiline once more a candidate for the consulship, Cicero got wind of suspicious goings-on. This time there really was a plot against the state. The information came from Fulvia, mistress of Quintus Curius, one of Catiline's fellow conspirators. Curius had blabbed to her that he would shortly be in the money, thus hoping to regain her affections at a time when his generosity to her had been dwindling because of his financial straits. She coaxed details out of him, and passed them on to Cicero. Without harder evidence, there was not a great deal that he could do, but he managed to have the elections postponed. When he taxed Catiline in the senate about the rumours, Catiline, hoping to bring senators round to his side, answered in riddles: ' "What am I doing wrong, when there are two bodies, one withered and decayed, but with a head, and the other headless, but strong and big, and I put myself at the head of the latter?" ' (Plutarch, *Cicero* 14).

Catiline's election promise was to cancel all debts. This bold step would doubtless appeal to many army veterans who could not make a living out of agriculture, to members of the nobility who were substantially in the red, such as was Catiline himself, and to overambitious politicians who were operating on credit, such as certainly was Caesar. It did not appeal to most members of the senate and the equestrian order, or to shopkeepers. The postponed elections passed peacefully, though Cicero attended wearing a breastplate under his tunic, which he made sure that the crowds could see. Caesar was easily elected praetor, but Catiline failed again: Lucius Licinius Murena and Decimus Junius Silanus were to be consuls in 62 BC.

Cicero went on piecing together evidence, with which he was able to persuade the senate that a wide-spread conspiracy was being organized. On 21 October 63 BC, the senate issued a *senatus consultum ultimum*. Overnight on 6 November Cicero learned that there was a plan to assassinate him and other leading members of the establishment the following morning, set the city on fire, and loot property; at the same time an army of Catiline's supporters, under Gaius Manlius, who had fought with distinction under Sulla, would march on Rome. Catiline would appear as if in response to the needs of both his followers and his opponents, and be appointed dictator. None of these things happened. Cicero called a meeting of the senate, which Catiline brazenly attended, though no-one would sit anywhere near him. Cicero made a blistering attack on him face to face. That night Catiline left the city to join Manlius. The senate formally declared them, and their army of 10,000, enemies of the state.

The conspirators still in the city betrayed themselves by making advances to a diplomatic mission from the Gallic Allobroges which was then in Rome, with a view to getting the tribe's support for Catiline. The Allobroges passed on this information to Cicero, who asked them to obtain signed letters from the conspirators confirming the approach. Armed with these, Cicero had five of Catiline's accomplices arrested. Among them was Publius Cornelius Lentulus Sura, consul in 79 BC, who had been expelled from the senate the following year, and was now rising through the ranks again, being praetor for 63 BC; he was also Mark Antony's stepfather.

Cicero called a meeting of the senate to debate their fate. He opened the proceedings by implying that he would support the death penalty. One after another, the consuls-elect and the former consuls agreed with him. Then Cicero invited Caesar, as praetor-elect, to speak.

For Caesar, too, the year 63 BC had been politically productive. He was active in the law courts, prosecuting the consul of 67 BC, Gaius Calpurnius Piso, for his treatment of a Transpadane Gaul during his subsequent governorship. Gaius Piso, whose defence lawyer was Cicero, was acquitted, but Caesar had been publicly seen to take the side of the Transpadane Gauls, whose enfranchisement he supported.

He also presided as a judge in a bizarre case which had an extraordinary ending. The defendant, Gaius Rabirius, was accused of killing the tribune Saturninus 37 years before, on the grounds that he was one of the young men on the roof throwing tiles down at those trapped inside. The case was not, however, about the identity of the murderer so much as the status of the victim, and the validity under the circumstances of the *senatus consultum ultimum* which appeared to justify the killing. Was the life of a tribune still sacrosanct in the face of a senatorial decision? Caesar thought it was, and passed the statutory sentence of death, knowing that Rabirius was entitled to appeal to the people against it. It was probably Caesar, too, having established his point of principle in law, who arranged for the appeal proceedings to be abandoned, and thus the whole case to be dissolved, by resorting to an archaic practice. From time immemorial a red flag had been flown on the Janiculum Hill. It was lowered in early republican days to warn the city of an impending attack by the Etruscans, and when the signal was given all public meetings must stop. Now, Quintus Metellus Celer, praetor in that year, had the flag lowered, and the court broke up.

In allowing the case against Rabirius, Caesar had been working in concert with Titus Labienus, who reappears in our narrative as tribune for that year. It was almost certainly at Caesar's instigation that Labienus now had a bill passed restoring to the constitution the *lex Domitia* of 104 BC, by which priests were elected by popular vote rather than appointed by their college, as Sulla had decreed. For Caesar had decided to risk his reputation by standing as a candidate for the office of *pontifex maximus*, rendered vacant by the death of Metellus Pius, who had held it since 80 BC.

The *pontifex maximus* was titular head of the religion of the state, and, by reason of the fact that it was occupied for life, it was the most prestigious office in the constitution, with which went a palatial residence in the middle of the forum. It was usually held by elderly statesmen of long political experience, and standing against Caesar were Lutatius Catulus, who should normally have been easily the favourite, and Servilius Vatia, consul in 79 BC and Caesar's former superior in the east. For Caesar, the office of *pontifex maximus* was merely a means to an end; it was not the end itself, as it was to his two opponents, of whom Catulus even tried unsuccessfully to bribe Caesar to withdraw. Caesar was only half way up the *cursus honorum*, but he had undoubted charm and persuasiveness, and he also had Crassus's money.

No doubt in his electioneering addresses from the *rostra* Caesar stressed his divine descent and the fact that he had been intended as *flamen dialis*. He also

*Figure 3.1* A procession of priests, from the *Ara Pacis*, some wearing distinctive leather caps with inverted spikes on the crown of the head. (C. M. Dixon/ Ancient Art & Architecture Collection)

resorted to massive bribery of the electorate, who would vote in the tribal assembly. What made the situation tricky was that in order to retain an essence of religious mystery about the proceedings in priestly elections, on the day only 17 out of 35 tribes, chosen by lot, cast their votes. Caesar was then living in a house in the Subura, an unprepossessing, noisy district of the city where provisions were sold and prostitutes plied their trade. On voting day it was not Pompeia, but his mother, in tears, who accompanied him to the door. 'He kissed her, and said, "Mother, today you'll see me either high priest or finished, an exile!" ' (Plutarch, *Caesar* 7).

Caesar won a landslide victory. To the *dignitas* (rank, prestige, honour) of the Julii, was now added the *dignitas* attached to this high office of state. It was certainly not any religious connotations of the office which attracted Caesar to it. As befitted a realist in war and an opportunist in politics, he was not averse to enjoying the material proceeds of religious office, while in practice taking little notice of the implications of the rituals. Along with other senior officers of state, he was invested with *auspicium*, the authority in this case to take the omens on public occasions. Yet he went into battle whether or not the sacred chickens had eaten their grain, or whatever colours the calves' livers were. On one memorable occasion, when a priest reported that the sacrificial beast was missing a heart, he observed, ' "The omens will be more favourable when I wish them to be" ' (Suetonius, *Julius Caesar* 77).

In August, known then as Sextilis, the sixth month of the original year, which began in March, Caesar, in his official capacity, attended a banquet to celebrate the inauguration of Mucius Lentulus Niger as *flamen Martialis*, priest of Mars. The house was profusely decorated. The couches on which the guests reclined were inlaid with ivory. Priests, including Caesar, occupied two of them. A third was reserved for women: Publicia, wife of the new *flamen*, Sempronia, his mother-in-law, and four vestal virgins. The menu survives in an early fifth-century AD miscellany:

> For starters: sea urchins, raw oysters, as many as you wanted, giant mussels, sea-food, thrushes dressed with asparagus, force-fed chicken, mussel and oyster pie, black and white sea-mussels, more varieties of sea-food, fig-peckers, loin of goat, saddle of boar, floured chicken pieces, purple shellfish. As main courses: sows' udders, boar's head, fish pie, mutton pie, duck, boiled teal, hare, roasted fowl, cakes, Picene pastries.
>
> Macrobius, *Saturnalia* III, 13

Meals such as this became commonplace in imperial times. One thing is certain, though: of all the guests on this occasion, the one sure to be at his desk at dawn the next morning, when the working day began, was Caesar.

When, on 5 December 63 BC, Caesar stood up to speak in the debate on the punishment of Catiline's co-conspirators, he had already been accused earlier in the senate by Lutatius Catulus, smarting under his defeat in the polls, of complicity in the plot. There is a full report of Caesar's impassioned, dignified, and meticulously argued speech, drawing on Greek as well as Roman historical precedents, in Sallust's *War of Catiline*, written within 25 years of the event. Though Sallust (*c.* 86–35 BC) was pro-Caesar, and served in his administration, there is no reason to doubt its accuracy. For one of his principal sources of information was Cicero, and on the day itself Cicero had discreetly disposed around the senate-house a number of his slaves who were skilled shorthand writers.

Caesar argued that instead of the accused being executed, their estates should be confiscated, and they should be imprisoned for life in various of the bigger towns in Italy, without anyone ever being allowed to appeal on their behalf. As for the death penalty,

> We can simply state the facts: in affliction and distress, death is not a torment but a relief from suffering; it is the end of all human misfortunes, beyond which there is no place for grief, or joy.
>
> Sallust, *War of Catiline* 51

On the face of it, this was an extraordinary statement from the head of the religion of the state, which held that the spirits of the dead lived on in the form of *manes* and *lemures*. To the Romans, however, impiety was not so much disrespect to the gods, but to the rituals through which they were worshipped. Whatever personal religious doubts Caesar may have had, and they would have been shared by other intellectuals, notably those who were adherents to the Epicurean school of philosophy, his position was unassailable as long as he observed the rituals.

When it seemed that Caesar was bringing members of the senate round to his way of thinking, Cicero called on Marcus Porcius Cato, tribune-elect, to address the house. He was known as Cato 'from Utica' to distinguish him from his eminent great-grandfather, Cato the 'Censor', with whom he shared an implacable nature, a stern moralistic sense, and a gift for oratory. He was a staunch supporter of the *optimates*, and an enemy of Caesar. Predictably, he reinforced the arguments for the death penalty, and predictably he won the day, but not before there had been a moment of drama and farce.

While Cato was speaking, a messenger brought in a note and handed it to Caesar. Cato halted his harangue, and accused Caesar of communicating with the conspirators. He then challenged Caesar to read the note out aloud, and several other senators voiced their support of his demand. Instead Caesar coolly handed it across to him, and sat down again while Cato read it. It was a love-letter from Cato's own half-sister, Servilia, Caesar's long-standing mistress. Cato threw it back at Caesar with the words, ' "Take it, you drunken sot!" ' (Plutarch, *Cato the Younger* 24). Then he resumed his speech.

When Caesar realized that the vote was going to go against him, he tried to block the proceedings, until a group of *equites*, employed as senatorial security guards, drew their swords, and ushered him out. For the remaining days of the year, Caesar kept away from the senate.

The vote was unanimous, but notwithstanding the *senatus consultum ultimum*, strictly it had no force in law: such decisions of the senate were only recommendations. Nevertheless, the accused were collected under guard from the praetors' homes where they had been kept under house arrest. Cicero himself accompanied Lentulus to the state prison, where people assumed the five prisoners would be kept until there had been a formal decision about their fate. Lentulus was let down into a small, stinking dungeon, and strangled. The other four were executed, one by one, in the same manner.

It was Cicero's finest hour.

CATO

# 4

# PRAETOR AND CONSUL 62–59 BC

As Caesar was crossing the Alps [to take up his post as governor in Spain in 61 BC], it is said that he passed a wretched village, occupied by a few barbarians. His companions made a joke of it: 'Could it be that here too there is rivalry for office, enmity over who should take precedence, and mutual jealousy between men of power?' To which Caesar answered, quite seriously, 'I would rather be first among these people than second in Rome.'

Plutarch, *Caesar* 11

Caesar's year as praetor began with his being suspended from office, and ended in scandal.

He had already, on 1 January 62 BC, caused offence by using his official powers to call a *contio* (public meeting), at which he ordered an enquiry into the lack of progress made by Lutatius Catulus, who was responsible for the rebuilding of the great temple of Jupiter on the Capitol Hill, which had burned down in 83 BC. Caesar also demanded an investigation into where the money had gone, and proposed that the assignment should be transferred to someone else. Though Catulus had dedicated a replacement of a sort in 69 BC, an occasion which he celebrated with 10 days of games, the building itself was still unfinished. Caesar's action, however, was probably no more than an exercise of spite against a man who had accused him in the senate of being a

48

supporter of Catiline. When Catulus's senatorial friends and colleagues arrived from celebrating the inauguration of the new consuls, Caesar adjourned the meeting *sine die*.

His next public demonstration was more serious. Quintus Metellus Nepos, half-brother of Pompey's wife Mucia and now serving as one of Pompey's legionary commanders, had been given home leave to act as Pompey's special envoy and, in particular, to stand as tribune for 62 BC in order to promote Pompey's interests. Now in office, he proposed that Pompey be given the job of ridding the state finally of Catiline and what remained of his followers, though the matter was already well in hand. It is possible that Nepos had a second proposal up his sleeve, that Pompey should be allowed to stand *in absentia* as a candidate for the consulship in 61 BC. Be that as it may, Cato, as tribune, announced that he would veto any such measures. Caesar gave notice that he supported them.

The stage was set for a showdown when voting took place on Nepos's bills, which would be read out from the steps of the temple of Castor and Pollux, with Caesar as presiding officer. When Caesar and Nepos had taken their places, Cato and his colleague Minucius Thermus marched up and seated themselves between them, so that they could not communicate with each other. Then, as the clerk began to declaim Nepos's measures, Cato pronounced the veto. Nepos took the scroll from the clerk, and began to read from it aloud. Cato snatched it away. Nepos, who knew the script by heart, carried on without it. Thermus tried to stop him by putting his hand over Nepos's mouth.

At this point, Nepos called up his hired thugs. They rained sticks and stones on Cato, who stood his ground until one of the consuls, Licinius Murena, sheltered him with his toga and persuaded him to take refuge in the temple. Nepos now proposed that the vote should proceed, but the supporters of Cato, who had dispersed at the first hint of violence, returned and shouted him down.

The senate now passed a *senatus consultum ultimum* and suspended from office not only Nepos, but also Caesar. The latter's punishment may be connected with whatever action he did, or did not, take during the fracas on the temple steps. It may also be that, as Suetonius suggests, he delivered a speech in the senate justifying what had been done and renewing his support for Nepos's proposals. According to Cassius Dio, these also included an official denunciation of the senate for condemning the associates of Catiline to death without the consent of the people.

Nepos returned to Pompey. Caesar at first refused to accept his exclusion, but sense prevailed, or he saw a way of making capital out of the incident. He took off his praetor's toga, with its stripe of Tyrian purple (actually a pinkish red), dismissed his lictors, the guards who walked in front of officials of state carrying the symbols of power, and went home. The next day, a noisy crowd gathered, probably not spontaneously, outside the house, calling for his reinstatement. Caesar went out and begged the demonstrators to desist. The senate was hastily convened. Caesar was thanked for his dignified behaviour, and invited to resume office.

Catiline was finally brought to battle, and defeated and killed, in February 62 BC. The fallout from his machinations, however, continued to haunt the senate, as efforts were made to root out, and punish, those who had any connections with him. It was a situation made for informers. Lucius Vettius, a friend of Catiline who had already given information to Cicero, now formally handed to Novius Niger, examiner in the criminal courts, a list of conspirators which included the name of Caesar. He also declared that he could produce a letter to Catiline written by Caesar. In the senate, Quintus Curius, who had been promised a reward from the public purse for being, if unwittingly, the original source of information, produced another list, also including the name of Caesar. Caesar reacted quickly and harshly, though within his rights, to what he claimed were assaults on the *dignitas* and *imperium* of his office.

In a trenchant speech to the senate he vigorously denied the allegation on the grounds that he had himself volunteered information about the plot to Cicero, who confirmed that this was so. Caesar also persuaded the assembled members to refuse to pay Curius his reward. As for Vettius, Caesar used his legal powers to declare forfeit the bond he had deposited when he made his allegations, and to seize his household goods. He then sent him to gaol, but not before Vettius had been beaten up in the forum by an angry crowd. Caesar also imprisoned Novius Niger, for allowing an official of higher rank than himself to be accused in his court.

The rest of Caesar's year of office seemed to be passing uneventfully until a disgraceful episode disrupted his personal life and was for several months, if not years, the talking point of Roman society. The festival of Bona Dea, the 'good goddess', was celebrated in the first week of December each year at the house of a senior official of the state. It was a mystical ceremony, involving secret rites and a certain amount of merriment, and was strictly for women only; men were not allowed even to be in the same building. In 62 BC, the venue was Caesar's house, the official residence of the *pontifex maximus*. A few days before taking office as quaestor, Publius Clodius Pulcher, a notorious upper-class lout, decided to infiltrate the ceremony disguised as a lute-girl.

Clodius was the son of Appius Claudius Pulcher, consul in 79 BC. His sister Clodia was married to their cousin, Quintus Metellus Celer, while having a blazing affair with the young poet Catullus, who calls her Lesbia in his verses. Clodius was a toady and he was arrogant: serving in the east in 68/67 BC, he stirred up a mutiny against his commanding officer, Lucius Licinius Lucullus, who was his own brother-in-law, because of an apparent offence against his dignity.

There was a story, which may have originated later, that Clodius was in love with Caesar's wife Pompeia, and that his attempted intrusion into the mysteries was a way of engineering a meeting with her when her husband was out of the way and her mother-in-law was busy organizing the ceremonials. It is more likely that it was simply a prank. He was discovered, recognized, and thrown out of the house by Aurelia, who stopped the ceremonies and ordered the vestal virgins to repeat them all over again to avoid any offence to the goddess. The ladies of the nobility who were participating in the rites went home and told their husbands what had happened. Then the reverberations began.

The incident was discussed in the senate, whereupon Caesar sent his wife a verbal message that he had divorced her. When asked later why he had done this, he replied enigmatically, ' "My wife must not even be thought to be under suspicion" ' (Plutarch, *Caesar* 10). This does not need to mean suspicion that there was any kind of relationship with Clodius. It was quite enough for Caesar that the scandal was likely to run and run, and might well end up in court, with the wife of the *pontifex maximus* having to answer awkward questions. Nor did he wish to be involved in the controversy by association when he had other things on his mind, the most pressing of which were his debts.

The senate referred the matter to the pontifical college for a decision as to whether a crime had been committed. The college's response was that there had, without being specific as to its nature. The senate now had to move for a prosecution. The administration was so preoccupied with this business that there was a delay in assigning by lot the responsibilities for 61 BC to the praetors of the previous year, one of whom was Caesar. While the furore was raging in Rome, Pompey returned from the east, confounding those who feared that he might emulate the homecoming of Sulla. He dismissed his troops when they disembarked at Brundisium, and made his heroic way to Rome with only a small escort.

Pompey was granted permission to hold a triumph later in the year for his military successes. Otherwise he got a cool welcome from the senate and no doubt an even cooler one from his family and from the Metelli, for on the way home he had sent a note to Mucia demanding a divorce on the grounds of adultery, and requesting her to leave his house immediately. That his motives were as usual political would seem to be confirmed by the fact that on his return he proposed a double marriage alliance with the family of Cato, who, with Cicero, was potentially his most dangerous opponent in the senate. He would marry one of Cato's nieces, and his son Gnaeus would marry her sister. The two women were said to have been very much in favour of such advantageous matches, but Cato put his foot down, saying that he was not assailable via the bedroom.

It was not until March that the ex-praetors got their commands. Caesar was assigned the governorship of the province of Further Spain, for which he departed without waiting for the senate to confirm the appointment and grant him the necessary funds. He would have got away even sooner had not his main creditors, taking advantage of the interval between his laying down one office and taking up another, impounded his carriage and wagon train. Crassus was forced to come, or came, to the rescue by paying off the most importunate of them, and giving surety for a further enormous sum that has been calculated to have been about one-eighth of his entire capital.

Caesar was in Spain when the long-awaited trial of Clodius took place in an atmosphere of confusion, with accusations of corruption being levelled at the jury, who asked for, and obtained, the protection of the senate before giving their verdict. The charge was an unusual one, involving a change in the law before it could be brought. The crime of incest related not only to forbidden sexual relations, but also to sex with a vestal virgin, for which the punishment was to be beaten to death, and for her to be walled up alive. It appears that a codicil to the law was passed, extending it to cover anyone who invaded the rites of the Bona Dea. Aurelia and one of Caesar's sisters testified that the accused was in the house. Clodius's defence team, however, insisted that he was away from Rome at the time, and produced a local government official to prove it. Cicero, called, unusually, as a witness, demolished the alibi. A guilty verdict seemed assured, but Crassus bribed the jury, according to Cicero offering as extra inducements nights with certain ladies and introductions to youths of noble birth, and Clodius was acquitted by 31 votes to 25.

In terms of Caesar's objectives, to make money and to prepare the way for his election to the consulship for 59 BC, his tour of duty in Further Spain, which he knew from his quaestorship 10 years before, was an outstanding success. On his arrival, he wasted no time on administrative affairs, but waded into the bandits who infested the southern region of the province, having raised from local resources 10 new cohorts (about 5000 men) to augment the 20 allocated to him. According to Cassius Dio, the bandits had probably always been there, and could have been removed without trouble or publicity. This was not Caesar's way. He ordered them to leave their mountain hideouts and settle in the plains, claiming that their movements could then be more easily monitored. The truth was that he knew they would never obey the order, and he would thus have an excuse to take aggressive action and relieve them of their booty. This is precisely what happened.

There had now begun a glorious campaign against largely defenceless peoples, in the course of which Caesar discovered his talent for mounting large-scale military operations. When fugitives from early battles escaped to an island off the west coast, he called up ships from Cadiz and transported his whole army across the strait. The inhabitants, already short of food, gave in without a blow being struck. He now used his fleet to show off the strength of Rome in places occupied by independent local tribes. The people of Brigantium, who had apparently never before seen ships in such numbers, surrendered to him. Other towns followed suit. At the slightest provocation or, according to Suetonius, even where there was no provocation, Caesar removed as many valuables as he could. In these ways he made so much money from booty, tribute, and backhanders that he was able not only to supplement his troops' pay but also prudently to send sums back to the public treasury.

With an eye to the electorate in Rome, he eased the unhappy relations between debtors and creditors (who were mainly equestrians) by establishing that a creditor was legally entitled to two-thirds of the debtor's income until the debt was paid off. He had also stored up good will towards himself by appointing Lucius Cornelius Balbus as his adjutant general. Balbus, a native of Cadiz whom Caesar had known when he was quaestor, had subsequently acquired Roman citizenship and moved to Rome, where his wealth and political instinct made him an influential figure.

Having achieved what he had set out to do, Caesar returned to Rome in the summer of 60 BC without waiting for his successor to arrive. A triumph for his successes in the fields and seas of Further Spain, for which his soldiers had already acclaimed him *imperator*, would be good for his public image, and the senate duly granted him one. Would he, however, be allowed to enter the city before the triumph in order to present himself as a candidate for election as consul? Or could he, as Pompey had done in 71 BC, stand *in absentia*? The majority of the senate were happy that he should. Cato, however, by a supreme piece of filibustering, ensured that the motion was abandoned when night fell and the house had to adjourn. Caesar bowed to the inevitable and, in pursuit of the political career he had mapped out for himself, forfeited his triumph and entered the polls.

Among the other candidates were Marcus Bibulus, whom Caesar loathed (Bibulus was also Cato's son-in-law), and Lucius Lucceius, a former senior praetor and friend of Pompey. Caesar formed an ingenious electoral compact with Lucceius, whereby Lucceius provided cash which would be handed out to prospective voters in the names of them both. The *optimates*, fearing the consequences of Caesar having a tractable consular colleague, set up a campaign fund for Bibulus, whom they authorized to spend as much as Caesar and Lucceius on bribing the electorate. Even Cato had to admit that this was a justifiable means of preserving the constitution. In addition, in a gesture of pure spite, the *optimates* pushed a motion through the senate that after their year of office, the consuls for 59 BC, instead of the rich provincial pickings that were their due, should be responsible for the care of 'woodlands and mountain pastures' of Italy.

Caesar and Bibulus were elected. The republican constitution was designed to restrict the power and influence of the individual. Caesar was a clever enough politician to circumvent the system. He established an informal alliance with Pompey and Crassus that none of them would take any political action of which the others disapproved. This understanding is sometimes referred to as the First Triumvirate, which is a misnomer in that the literal meaning of triumvirate is 'rule (or board) of three'. It might still, though, have been four, if Cicero had responded favourably to an approach by Balbus, acting on Caesar's behalf, to join them. Cicero was vain and sometimes rather pompous; in a letter to his friend Atticus, he explained that his reason for refusing was enshrined in the third book of his poem about his consulship, being effectively to be true to one's original principles. By his refusal, however, he offended Caesar, Crassus, and Pompey.

Caesar had the charisma, the popular appeal, and, for the year 59 BC, the power; Crassus had the money; Pompey had the influence over his former troops. In return for money, votes, and moral support, Caesar promised Pompey that he would get through the senate the measures he wanted to provide land settlements for his veterans and official confirmation of the administrative arrangements that he had left in place in the province of Asia; to Crassus, he undertook to back measures proposed by the equestrians to renegotiate the Asian tax-collecting contracts on the grounds that those who had won them had bid too much.

Pompey was still, conveniently, a bachelor. Caesar bound himself even closer by giving him his daughter Julia in marriage. She was now about 17, and betrothed to somebody else, but politics spoke louder than priorities. Even so, and with Pompey some 30 years older than she was, it appears to have been an extraordinarily happy union, as long as it lasted. Caesar now called on his son-in-law instead of Crassus to open debates in the senate, though by tradition the same precedence should have been retained as had been established at the beginning of the year.

Maybe it was Julia moving out of the house which suggested to Caesar that he should now marry again. If his third wife, Calpurnia, married at the usual age of between 14 and 16, then she would have been younger than his daughter. Calpurnia's parents were Lucius Calpurnius Piso Caesoninus and Rutila. Calpurnius Piso was a man of distinction and intellect. He was the patron of the Epicurean philosopher Philodemus, who lived and gave seminars in the magnificent house known as the Villa of the Papyri which Piso built in Herculaneum. It is probable that the Pisos to whom the poet Horace (65 BC–8 BC) dedicated his *Ars Poetica* (The Art of Poetry) were his son, Lucius Piso, and Lucius Piso's two sons. Horace quotes in his *Satires* I. 2 an epigram of Philodemus, who was also tutor to Virgil (70–19 BC), the national poet of Rome. There is some evidence that Calpurnia shared her father's interest in Epicureanism, with its primitive atomic theory of the universe, and the beliefs that there was nothing to fear in God or from the supernatural, that death was the end of all things, that pleasure was the ultimate good, and that competition, deep emotional commitments, and conflict were to be avoided.

In some things anyway, Caesar would have found Calpurnia a sympathetic helpmate. Though there is no direct evidence that he subscribed to the philosophical doctrines of Epicurus (341–270 BC), he certainly displayed an Epicurean attitude to death and an Epicurean scepticism of the supernatural.

He could be described as a practising pragmatist, who regarded religion simply as an inseparable part of the political spectrum in which he was almost exclusively engaged.

Having done what he could to ensure some kind of following in the senate, it was necessary for Caesar also to have in his pocket one or more tribunes of the people. From those elected in December 60 BC, he selected as his principal mouthpiece Publius Vatinius, who apparently demanded so much in bribes for his services that Caesar remarked that during his year as a tribune Vatinius did nothing for nothing. Vatinius immediately made his presence felt by introducing a series of measures of his own, and by issuing a warning to the senate that he would take a dim view of any attempt to obstruct business by the invocation of omens.

Pompey's scholarly friend and mentor, Terentius Varro, defined the term consul as 'one who "consults" the people and the senate' (*On the Latin Language* V. 14). By the time of Caesar, convention and the will of the majority of members of the senate had reduced the functions of the consuls largely to formalities. Caesar took convention by the scruff of the neck and, in the interests of the people as well as of himself and his political allies, tore it to shreds. Appian refers to Caesar as a 'master of double talk' (*Civil Wars* II. 10). His initial speech in the senate, over which he was, as the consul who headed the poll, due to preside for the month of January, outwardly gave little indication of what was to come. His regulation that proper records should be made and published daily of all proceedings in the senate and the peoples' assemblies could be taken either as a freedom of information act or as a warning. He also assured his audience that, while working for the welfare of the people, he would propose nothing that would not also benefit the traditionalists in the senate.

He went on to explain that though he and Bibulus had had their differences, it was not in the interests of sound government that these should be brought out into the open. In February, however, when Bibulus took over from him, Caesar ingeniously demonstrated his contempt for his colleague. It was customary for the presiding consul to be preceded by 12 lictors, who walked before him one after the other in a line, each carrying the *fasces*, a bundle of rods with an axe in the middle, symbolizing the consul's *imperium* and the punishments that could be meted out to criminals. With a great show of ostentation, during February Caesar had a herald walk in front of him, while strung out behind him marched a train of lictors.

Caesar's first measure was a land bill which would resolve the pressing problem of Pompey's veterans and also do something to relieve overcrowding in Rome. Earlier attempts over the years had been defeated. Caesar worked on the original drafts so as to iron out any immediate objections. In particular, the cost of the lands was to be met from the booty Pompey had acquired in the east and from the new taxes from his reorganization of the provincial system there. The scheme would be run by a commission of 20, from which

Caesar was to be excluded, with an inner management committee of five. The result was a document ostensibly so flawless that Caesar's disgruntled opponents in the senate could find nothing with which publicly to disagree. So instead, they resorted to delaying tactics, and put up Cato to talk the bill out. Cato obliged, until, as sunset approached, Caesar, fearing that an adjournment would give his opponents time to marshal their thoughts and redeploy their resources, used his emergency powers to have him carted off to jail. Cato went quite readily. Numerous senators poured out in support of him; Marcus Petreius, who had had the distinction of finally defeating Catiline in the field, explained as he passed the chair of office that he would rather be in prison with Cato than in the senate with Caesar.

With the session now adjourned, Caesar abandoned the debate and took his bill direct to the *comitia centuriata*, as he did throughout the rest of the year with any measure he was himself promulgating. Before any vote was taken on a bill in a people's assembly, it was customary for a *contio* to be held in the forum at which the proposals could be discussed publicly. Caesar opened the proceedings by calling on Bibulus to speak. Bibulus announced that he had nothing to say on the matter except that he would oppose any new legislation during his term of office. Caesar appealed to the assembled crowd, explaining that without the assent of Bibulus, there would be no law. Bibulus bawled out, ' "You won't have this law this year, even if you all want it!" ' (Cassius Dio XXXVIII. 4).

Caesar thought better of asking any other elected officers of the state for their views, and instead invited Pompey and Crassus to speak. Pompey, who had most to gain from the measures, was very pleased to do so, and expounded at great length on the history of the bill, and explained each clause of it in detail. When Caesar saw that Pompey had got the crowd behind him, he asked Pompey whether he would help him against those who opposed the bill, urging the crowd to voice their support. At this Pompey, delighted with the popular response to the opinions of someone who was, after all, only a private citizen, launched into another long harangue, culminating with, ' "If anyone dares to draw his sword, I shall take up my shield too" ' (Cassius Dio XXXVIII. 5). Crassus spoke more briefly in support of Pompey's stance. Caesar fixed the day on which the count would take place. Pompey made the result a foregone conclusion by calling up his veterans to Rome, where they camped in the forum the night before the vote.

Thus was Caesar's first significant piece of legislation as consul passed by the people, but not before Bibulus had tried other means of obstructing the process of government such as have been described in Chapter 1. With Bibulus voluntarily incarcerated at home, Caesar was free to act on his own for the rest of the year. Various practical jokes went the rounds, such as signing off spoof documents with the phrase, 'Executed in the consulship of Julius and Caesar'.

A second land law extended the existing legislation to include in the scheme the 200 square miles of desirable Campanian countryside which belonged to the state. These initiatives of Caesar distributed land and space in which to live to many thousands of needy, if not also deserving, citizens of Rome, who would now be his political followers; Cicero referred to them as 'Caesar's army'. Caesar also kept his election promises with legislation to remit one-third of the money owed by the Asian tax-collectors (which pleased the equestrians and benefited those involved), and for Pompey's eastern commitments to be ratified (which benefited Pompey). He was in addition instrumental in the claim being accepted of Ptolemy XII to be officially recognized in Rome as king of Egypt. To achieve this, Ptolemy borrowed vast amounts of money, much of which found its way into the pockets of Caesar and Pompey. Caesar's *lex Julia de repetundis*, however, which regulated the financial powers of provincial governors, was more altruistic and remained in force for many years.

Caesar was not above silencing vocal opponents by quasi-legal means, even if it meant using Clodius Pulcher to do so. Clodius, balked by his reputation of obtaining political advancement through the channels available to patricians, had been trying to have his status changed to plebeian, in order to be able to stand for election as a tribune of the people. His efforts had been blocked by the action of his brother-in-law, Metellus Celer, as consul in 60 BC.

In March 59 BC, Gaius Antonius, Cicero's former consular colleague, was tried for extortion in a case that had the backing of Caesar and Crassus. Cicero undertook the defence, not so much out of duty but as a protest against the administration. Sure enough, in the course of a political diatribe about the evils of the present situation, he made a personal attack on Caesar's methods of obtaining results. That same afternoon, Clodius was enrolled, by adoption, in the ranks of the plebs.

Properly, the process required the formal assent of a public assembly. Caesar, as consul, fast-tracked the application. Approval was given by the *pontifex maximus* (Caesar again) in the presence of an augur (Pompey), who announced that the auspices were favourable. Clodius was then formally adopted by Publius Fonteius, a young man almost half his age, who immediately released him from his legal obligations to his new father, so that Clodius retained his former nomenclature. Cicero got the message, and left town for a tour of his various villas in the country.

Caesar's future, after his consular year, depended on his bizarre command over the 'woodlands and mountain pastures' being transmuted into something more influential, more powerful, and more profitable, and on such a smooth transfer of office that he could not, in any interval between, be brought to book for irregularities committed while he was consul. He decided what he wanted, and in May 59 BC Vatinius proposed to the people that with immediate effect Caesar should be responsible for the provinces of Cisalpine Gaul and Illyricum, with three legions and provision for their maintenance, until 1 March 54 BC. Since there could be no Roman troops in Italy south of the river Rubicon, which marked the border with Cisalpine Gaul, whoever governed the province effectively commanded the rest of Italy too, and was also within easy distance of Rome. If Caesar wanted military prestige, Illyricum offered a taking-off point for operations against the troublesome Dacians.

It was an extraordinary command, but it is possible that Caesar already had his sights on an even greater provincial prize. The Celtic tribes outside the frontiers of Transalpine Gaul had begun massing for trouble, among themselves and with Rome. Metellus Celer, consul in 60 BC, had been appointed governor of Transalpine Gaul, with a brief to prosecute the war against the tribes if necessary. In April 59 BC, before he had even left Rome, he died: some said he was poisoned by his wife Clodia, who, as well as her other flings, was having an affair, or was about to embark on an affair, with the playboy Marcus Caelius Rufus. In May, Pompey proposed in the senate that Caesar, as well as his existing provincial commitments, should be assigned Transalpine Gaul. Cato as usual blustered, sneering that daughters were being used as bargaining tools, and that the senate was being invited to put a tyrant in its citadel. The senate, however, realizing that it could be outflanked once again if the proposal was put to the people, conceded defeat. Caesar was given the extra command and an additional legion; this appointment was to run from 1 January 58 BC, on an annual renewable basis.

Clodius was duly elected tribune. In July, Cicero, now back in Rome, wrote to his friend Atticus, 'Nothing in my experience was ever so scandalous, so corrupt, so deeply offensive equally to all kinds, ranks, and ages as the present administration; it is far worse than I thought it would be, or even, good heavens, than I had wished it to be' (*To Atticus* II. 19). Bibulus, who comes down in history as the kind of public figure who gets everything wrong, was even being hailed as another Quintus Fabius Maximus, surnamed Cunctator (Delayer), whose masterly inactivity was said to have saved the state in the war against Hannibal. Cicero admitted, however, that Caesar had made him several offers, including a seat on the land commission. Caesar also invited Cicero to accompany him on his posting as his deputy. Cicero refused this too, though admitting that 'It would have been a more honourable way of avoiding danger' (*To Atticus* II. 19). At that, Caesar washed his hands of Cicero.

One of Caesar's most dangerous attributes was his legendary charm, which he exercised on men and women alike. Suetonius lists, among Caesar's noble-born mistresses, Postumia, wife of the lawyer Servius Sulpicius, Lollia, wife of Pompey's associate Aulus Gabinius, Tertulla, wife of Crassus, and even Pompey's wife Mucia. His favourite, however, was Servilia, Cato's half-sister. She was about the same age as Caesar. With Marcus Junius Brutus she had a son, also Marcus Junius Brutus, who had been brought up by Cato after his father's death and was now known as Quintus Caepio Brutus from an uncle who had formally adopted him. Servilia's second husband was Decimus Silanus, consul in 62 BC, whom she had married in 77 BC and with whom she had three daughters. Caesar was a connoisseur of pearls. One of his party tricks was to guess the value of one by weighing it in the palm of his hand. During his consulship he gave Servilia a pearl worth six million sesterces, that is the equivalent of the value of the property of Sextus Roscius that Sulla's freedman Chrysogonus had been so keen to get his hands on. It was even rumoured that Caesar had an affair with Servilia's daughter Tertia. Cicero made a neat Latin pun about Caesar's action later of giving Servilia a discount on estates confiscated and then auctioned after the subsequent civil war, when he said that Caesar had 'knocked off a third (*tertia*)' of the price.

While neither Crassus nor Pompey could claim to be a long-term strategist, to Caesar, the ultimate politician who coldly thought through every move, forward planning was his *raison d'être*. It was necessary for him, while he was away from Rome gaining prestige and glory, to protect not only his back but also his political future. Accordingly it was fixed that the consuls for 58 BC, elected the previous October, should be Aulus Gabinius, Pompey's man, and Calpurnius Piso, Caesar's father-in-law.

Someone, preferably as audacious and ruthless as he was himself, was required to act in Caesar's interests in the people's assemblies, especially as Vatinius, having completed his year in office as a tribune, was to accompany Caesar as a legionary commander. Caesar made a calculated, if risky, decision, and put his trust in the erratic, possibly unbalanced, demagogue, Publius Clodius, to neutralize his more vociferous opponents.

On 10 December 59 BC, the day the new tribunes took office, Clodius put forward four laws which subsequently passed into the statute book unopposed. The first two, concerning the procedure for the expulsion of a senator by the censors, and imposing a ban on senior officials (except tribunes) obstructing public business by invoking unfavourable omens, could be said to be reasonable measures. The other two were social dynamite, with implications unforeseen at the time. Since 64 BC, there had been restrictions on the formation and activities in the city of clubs or guilds, to prevent subversive gatherings. Clodius's bill removed the ban, and gave permission for new organizations to be formed. Clubs were now open not only to members of the poorer classes who could not afford the fees of the traditional guilds, but also to seditious and violent elements, who comprised the gangs which were to be manipulated for electoral purposes. In 62 BC, in the aftermath of the unease caused by Catiline, Cato had had a law passed which increased the benefits of the corn distribution among the poor and landless. Clodius, in a wildly popular and extravagant move, now made the distribution free, and extended it to all Roman citizens. Three hundred thousand members of the populace were now effectively to receive the dole, at a cost of about one-fifth of the revenue of the state.

At the close of the consular year, two praetors, Lucius Domitius Aheno-barbus, Cato's brother-in-law, and Gaius Memmius, who was a son-in-law of Sulla, questioned Caesar's consular regime on the grounds that he had acted unconstitutionally if not also illegally. The senate failed to agree on the motions, whereupon a tribune, Lucius Antistius, charged him to appear before the tribunes' court. Caesar declined the summons, claiming that he could not be prosecuted while away from Rome on business of state. To underline his point, he removed himself outside the sacred limits of the city, and awaited developments.

Clodius, meanwhile, was working on his next gambit. He announced two further measures. Following the precedent of Vatinius's law on Caesar's tenure of office after his consular year, he would propose that from 57 BC Calpurnius Piso and Aulus Gabinius should be granted five-year terms as governors respectively of the desirable provinces of Macedonia and Syria. Secondly he would reaffirm the law of Gaius Gracchus that sentences of death were the prerogative of the people, and that anyone who caused, or had caused, the execution of a citizen illegally should be banished.

Cicero, aghast, took off his official toga and resumed that of an equestrian, as he went about soliciting support for his cause. The equestrian order was behind him, but Clodius mustered his gangs to molest its members in the street. Caesar advised Cicero to leave the city if he wanted to live. Pompey kept promising his help, but when it came to the crunch always managed to be out of town at the crucial moment. Clodius hated Cicero anyway, because of the humiliation he had suffered at his hands at the Bona Dea trial. He now used the political device of the *contio* to bring matters to a head, and called a public meeting in the Circus Flaminius. As it was outside the city limits, Caesar could make a personal appearance.

Clodius first invited the consuls to speak on the motion to reimpose the law of Gaius Gracchus. Piso, who was primarily a man of peace, spoke of his aversion to the execution of criminals outside the law, and when specifically asked by Clodius about the case under discussion, replied, ' "No deed of cruelty pleases me" ' (Cassius Dio XXXVIII. 16). It is probable that he would have said the same even if he had not already been bribed to do so by Clodius's earlier provision. Gabinius echoed Piso's sentiments, without putting in any good word for Cicero. Caesar was then invited to address the company. His speech was his usual masterpiece of political discretion. He alone, he reminded his audience, while accepting the guilt of Lentulus and his associates, had held out against their execution without legal trial. He did not necessarily agree, however, that any law should be applied retrospectively. On the other hand, by his offer of the position in Gaul he had given his friend Cicero a way out of his present difficulties, which had been refused.

That took care of Cicero. He had already left the country when he was formally banished 400 miles from Rome. His house in Rome was confiscated, and then destroyed by Clodius's mob.

A more elaborate stratagem was needed to dispense with Cato. Clodius achieved this by annexing to the Roman empire the island of Cyprus, which was ruled by Ptolemy, brother of the king of Egypt. The grounds for this were trivial and had to do with an incident years before when Clodius had been captured by local pirates, and Ptolemy had failed to come up with enough ransom money. This done, Clodius had another law passed, appointing Cato ambassador extraordinary to the Cypriot court, with the powers of a praetor. That took care of Cato.

As Caesar rode off to begin his assignment as governor and military commander over three provinces, he could, now that his two most able adversaries were temporarily out of the way, pursue with greater peace of mind his intricate vision of himself at the centre of the known world.

CRASSUS

# 5

# THE GENERAL
## Gaul and Britain 58–55 BC

[Caesar] longed for a high command, a great army, and a pioneering war in which his brilliant qualities could be demonstrated.

Sallust, *War of Catiline* 54

The predominantly Celtic tribes of Gaul maintained a loose, sometimes adversarial, relationship with each other. Though they had not developed the art of writing, they had other skills, such as metal work, weapon-making, and agriculture, to a high degree. They had natural resources and they had space. There were opportunities for trade and the manufacture of Roman goods. An enforced colonization would enable the Romans to emerge out of the restrictions imposed by the narrow land of Italy, while at the same time extending the buffer zone between Rome and the dangerous tribes of Germany. There is, therefore, some economic and social, as well as political, justification for Caesar's campaigns in Gaul.

That we know so much, and in such detail, about these campaigns is due to Caesar's ability as a writer, his need to keep his name before the public, and his general flair for publicity. Modern scholarship has concluded that the seven books of *De Bello Gallico* (The Gallic War) were compiled as a serial publication to promote his image among Roman citizens not only in Rome itself, but also in the Roman towns and colonies of Italy. No doubt in written form they were meant also to supplement his dispatches to the senate. They were certainly intended to counter the military fame and political reputation of Pompey, who, though a patron of literature, never wrote a book in his life.

The impact of the first seven books of *The Gallic War* (sometimes referred to as Caesar's 'commentaries') helped to ensure that he had no time, nor any need, to complete the history of these campaigns – an eighth book was added after Caesar's death by his officer, Aulus Hirtius, who in his dedication, addressed to Balbus, offers a literary appreciation which may not be far off the mark:

> Everyone else knows how smoothly he wrote, and without any cor-
> rections; we know, too, how easily and how quickly he finished these
> works. Caesar was not only a superb stylist, but was truly skilled in
> explaining his stratagems.
>
> Aulus Hirtius, *The Gallic War* VIII. Dedication

Caesar did not need a ghost writer. He was also the author of a two-volume work, now lost, which he dictated while crossing the Alps. This was *De Analogia*, a treatise on grammar, incorporating comments on orthography, phonology, conjugations of verbs, and aspirates, and setting out rules for forming and declining nouns and participles. Plutarch describes Caesar travelling by carriage with a slave wedged in beside him taking dictation, and comments that on his first trip from Rome to Gaul (a distance of over 700 miles), he went so fast that he reached the river Rhône in seven days. According to Aulus Gellius, Caesar's literary credo was to eschew unusual words and extravagant language as one would avoid rocks at sea.

There are two groups of manuscripts of *The Gallic War*, both dating from between the tenth and the twelfth centuries AD. When one allows for Caesar's requirement to put himself centre stage, to play up his own actions, and also those of his centurions and ordinary legionaries, and to play down those of his more senior officers, except for their getting themselves into difficulties from which he then rescued them, the result is an honest but also dramatic narrative, written in the third person. One may imagine Caesar, at the end of each season, writing up these accounts from his campaign notes, which had as likely as not been dictated on horseback to two or more secretaries at once. His finished scripts would be despatched to his personal information and publicity office in Rome, which was under the charge of Balbus and Gaius Oppius. Copies would be made and distributed wherever in Italy a crowd could be encouraged to gather to hear Caesar's words being declaimed.

The first people to show in Gaul in 58 BC were the Helvetii, who occupied the region equivalent to modern Switzerland. They felt threatened not only by Germanic tribes across the Rhine, but also by their Gallic neighbours, the Aedui and Sequani. As other peoples of the ancient world did in similar circumstances, they decided on a vast migration, aiming to settle towards the west-facing coast of Gaul. There were two possible routes, of which the easier was to cross the Rhône by bridge at Geneva, and take themselves through the territory of the Allobroges, which bordered on the province of Transalpine Gaul, and then through the province itself.

Caesar's scouts could hardly miss the preparations. Thousands of migrants (Caesar later claimed that they numbered 263,000), nobles, wise men, farmers, craftsmen, warriors, and their families, with their animals and ox-wagons, began to muster at the Rhône crossing, where a grand assembly had been called for 28 March of the Helvetii and associated tribes who were to make the journey. Caesar, having travelled direct from Rome to Geneva by express carriage, had the bridge destroyed, and awaited developments. The Helvetii sent an embassy to him, to request permission to travel through the province. Caesar, who had available only the one legion (about 5000 men) which garrisoned Transalpine Gaul, played for time, and asked them to return in a week. He then used his legionaries, assisted by auxiliary troops, to construct in the Rhône valley, between the lake of Geneva and the Jura mountains, 18 miles of fortified wall, 5 metres high, with a trench in front.

He was now able to inform the Helvetii that to traverse Roman property was against precedent, and that any attempt to do so would be met with force. The Helvetii tried to cross the river on rafts and storm the defences on the other side, but were stopped by hails of missiles. Eventually they gave up, and determined to try the northern route, along much narrower tracks through the territory of the Sequani and the Aedui. To Caesar, this still constituted a threat. He set off himself for Cisalpine Gaul, leaving his deputy, the experienced campaigner Titus Labienus, in charge. One wonders at this point how Cicero would have fared in this post, or even whether Caesar ever seriously intended him to have it.

In Cisalpine Gaul, Caesar speedily mobilized the other three regular legions under his command, which had been in winter quarters in Aquileia, the fortress town which guarded routes in and out of Italy to the north east. He also raised two more legions from the locals. This was illegal as legionaries had to be Roman citizens, a privilege not yet afforded to the Cisalpine Gauls. When needs must, however, Caesar was never one to play strictly by the rules. With a series of forced marches, he joined up again with Labienus. By this time, the Helvetii had passed through the territory of the Sequani. Now, their slow-moving line of packed humanity was causing problems to the Aedui and also to the Allobroges, who had only recently been conquered by Rome. The Aedui and Allobroges appealed to Caesar for help. This was precisely the kind of justification for which he was looking.

The Helvetii were even now reported to be crossing the river Saône over a pontoon bridge. Three-quarters of them had reached the other side. Caesar swooped on the rest, as they were preparing to cross, slaughtering many and putting the others to flight. It was a famous victory, in a way. These Helvetii represented the tribal division called the Tigurini, who in 107 BC, during the Roman wars against the Cimbri and Teutones, had sallied out on their own and ignominiously defeated a Roman army, killing its consul and his military commander, Lucius Piso, who was Calpurnia's great-grandfather.

Armies of the republic were commanded by men who were primarily politicians. They may have had practical army experience as military tribunes, legionary legates, or provincial governors, but no formal training. As a young man, Caesar had demonstrated courage and resourcefulness in the field, two of the many qualities required by a successful general. As governor in Spain he had mounted some notable operations against minimal opposition. He would have read the Greek historians, particularly Polybius (c. 200–c. 118 BC), who was a former cavalry commander of the Achaean league of states in 170/69 BC and subsequently became adviser to Scipio Aemilianus Africanus, in whose company he was when Scipio destroyed Carthage in 146 BC. Polybius wrote a study of tactics and a history of the war against Numantia, whose final defeat, engineered by Scipio, was witnessed by Marius. His *magnum opus*, however, was a history of the rise of Rome to world power in a matter of fifty years, and of how that power was exercised.

At different times, Caesar had up to ten legionary legates, appointed by himself, of whom the senior, with the rank of praetor, was Labienus. These could be, and under Caesar were, assigned to command one or more legions, as the situation demanded. Over the course of the Gallic wars, two men, Marcus Crassus, elder son of Crassus, and Mark Antony, are named as quaestor, which has been taken to be the equivalent of quartermaster-general, in charge of finance and supplies. They could also be given commands over legions in the field. Two other senior officers are mentioned, both young men. Publius Crassus, younger brother of Marcus Crassus, distinguished himself in action as a commander of auxiliary cavalry. Decimus Junius Brutus demonstrated some initiative in the job, probably an unenviable one for an army man, of commanding Caesar's battle fleet.

There is no suggestion in his commentaries, or anywhere else, that at any time on campaign Caesar sought or was given any advice; indeed it was usually he who showed his men what to do, whether it was standing with them in the line of battle or instructing his engineers how to cut off a town's water supply. He did employ men at various times whose function it was to furnish him with specialist advice in Rome or from Rome: Balbus on the political situation, Oppius on publicity, and Gaius Trebatius on legal matters. As far as the Gallic wars were concerned, however, even Labienus is represented as someone who simply takes orders, except on the occasion when he advises Caesar that he cannot not join him with his legion, because on balance it is unsafe to do so; Caesar shows grudging approval, which gives him the opportunity to point out to his audience that he now embarked on that particular mission with only two legions instead of three, and still succeeded, of course.

While, according to his commentaries, Caesar took the credit for everything, he also seems to have taken responsibility for almost everything, including his own mistakes. They also reveal, however, his preoccupation with problems of supply, highlighting the judgment required when balancing the tactical need for a sudden strike, with a force marching light, against the difficulties of feeding the men. He was everything a true Roman should be, always looking to take the initiative, but above all he was resourceful and, in the same way as all great generals, he believed in himself, and luck was on his side.

Caesar started the campaign with four legions. He raised four more from his own provinces in 58/57 BC, which he paid for himself until 56 BC. He subsequently raised an additional four, whose pay and equipment he financed personally. The backbone of the legion was its centurions, each of whom commanded 80 men. With his soldiers, Caesar was strict and correct, and he trained and worked them hard. They were loyal to him because they trusted and respected him. He always ensured that his men were properly rewarded with loot, which was carefully hoarded for them in the baggage train, and with slaves. In 51 BC, after much of a winter spent harassing the local population here, there, and everywhere by a series of forced marches, Caesar promised each man a bonus in lieu of booty equivalent to six months' pay.

Having destroyed about a quarter of the Helvetian line of march, now he had to devise some means of tackling the rest. The Aedui were not a united tribe. The leader of one group, Diviciacus, was, according to Cicero, who met him in Rome, a druid, one of the priestly class; he favoured relations with Rome. His brother Dumnorix secretly backed the Helvetii, from whom he had received assurances of support. Caesar sent after the Helvetii his 4000 auxiliary cavalry, enlisted in Gaul from the tribes. The Helvetii, with a troop of only 500, put them to flight. Caesar received intelligence that the panic had been deliberately engineered by Dumnorix, commanding the Aeduan detachment of cavalry, and that Dumnorix had also been sabotaging the deliveries of corn from local farmers to the army. Having discovered that these charges were true, Caesar made a political decision; it was more important to him to retain the support of Diviciacus, who pleaded for his brother, than to punish Dumnorix, whom, however, he kept under close watch.

The corn situation, thanks to Dumnorix, was pretty dire, so Caesar was forced to break off his pursuit and make for Bibracte, the chief town of the Aedui, to obtain supplies. The Helvetii, interpreting the move as a retreat, came after him. The confrontation was Caesar's first experience of a set-piece battle. It was a triumph for tactical inspiration and Roman discipline.

Caesar drew up his four regular legions on the downward slope of a hill in the classic Roman formation of three lines, each eight men deep, in front of

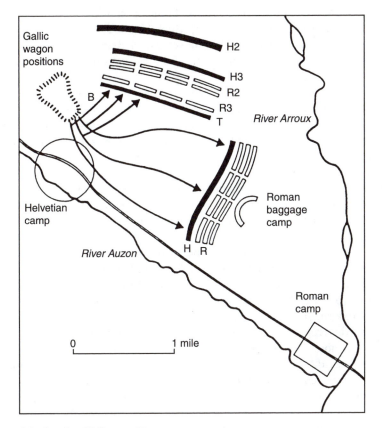

*Plan 1*: The battle of Bibracte 58 BC

Caesar drew up his legions in three lines (R). The Helvetii, in close-packed columns, advanced and attacked (H), but were thrown into confusion by the Roman javelins. Then Caesar advanced. The Helvetii retired to a hill to the north (H2). Caesar wheeled to face them, but was attacked in the rear by the Boii and Tulungi (B, T). The first two Roman lines remained facing the Helvetii (R2), who returned to the attack (H3). The third Roman line faced about (R3). Both enemy forces were defeated.

the baggage camp. With a truly Roman gesture, he sent away his horse and ordered his officers to do the same, thus denying himself an elevated view of the battlefield. When the fighting began, his javelin fire dispersed the massed ranks of Helvetii, who withdrew to a neighbouring hill slope and rallied. The Romans advanced against them in formation, only to be attacked from the rear by 15,000 warriors of the tribes of the Boii and Tulungi, who were part of the migration but had not so far been involved in the hostilities. Calmly, Caesar ordered his third line to about-turn, while his two front ranks still engaged the Helvetii. The result, after the main battle had lasted until dusk, was total victory on both fronts. Fighting continued into the night, however, round the Helvetian wagons, which had been moved into defensive positions. From behind these the Helvetii hurled missiles, or discharged javelins and darts from underneath the vehicles, causing further casualties, until they, too, were overrun.

According to Caesar, 130,000 survivors limped away towards the territory of the Lingones, leaving the Romans in possession of the wagons, the baggage, and the camp, where they took into custody some valuable non-combatant prisoners. He sent despatches to the Lingones, ordering them not to help the Helvetii in any way, or give them food. He and his army followed three days later, having buried their dead and tended the wounded. As he expected, the Helvetii, without provisions, begged for mercy. Caesar demanded hostages, the surrender of weapons, and the return of slaves who had deserted; then he announced his decision with regard to the rest.

> He told the Helvetii, Tulungi, and Latobrigi to return within their own borders, from which they had come, and since they had lost all their provisions and had nothing at home, he instructed them to be given by the Allobroges a generous allowance of corn. He also ordered them to repair the towns and settlements that they had burned en route. His principal reason for sending them back was that he did not want the region from which they had come to remain unoccupied, in case the Germans on the other side of the Rhine should be tempted by the rich farmland to come across from their territory to that of the Helvetii, and become neighbours of the province of Gaul and of the Allobroges. He agreed that the Aedui might house within their own borders the Boii, whose reputation for courage was formidable. The Aedui gave them farm land, and later granted them the same rights to justice and freedom as they had themselves.
>
> Caesar, *The Gallic War* I. 28

If Caesar composed *The Gallic War* seven years after this incident, as was formerly assumed, it could be passed over as probably described with hindsight. Now that he appears to have been writing for serial publication, it may be construed as an exercise of remarkable diplomacy at such an early stage of his campaign. And the Boii remained true to Rome, after their fashion.

The next stage of Caesar's campaign virtually fell into his lap, though he had to exercise some ingenuity to justify the justification. Diviciacus, as spokesman for the tribal chiefs of Gaul, officially drew to his attention the potential threat of a full-scale invasion by Ariovistus, chief of the Suebi, a Germanic tribe east of the Rhine. Caesar was well aware of the danger, and also of the diplomatic problem. In 59 BC, with Caesar's acquiescence, Ariovistus had been officially dubbed 'friend of the Roman people' for resolving by force of arms a dispute which had originally developed between the Aedui and the Sequani. Now he was settling his people rather too enthusiastically on lands to the west of the Rhine to which he was not fully entitled.

Caesar quickly exhausted initial diplomatic exchanges by making demands which he knew Ariovistus could hardly accept. Ariovistus now moved to take Vesontio, chief town of the Sequani. Caesar needed to get there first, because it had an abundant supply of arms and munitions, and was well situated to be the command centre of a campaign. He achieved this, and still had time to spend a few days replenishing his food supplies before he needed to set out again after Ariovistus. He was all ready to go, however, when there was panic in the army at the thought of meeting the fearsome Germans, reports of whose size, strength, and military prowess were being circulated by local Gauls and traders. According to Caesar, the trouble started with those military tribunes who were political appointees with no great experience of war; it then spread to all ranks. He summoned all his centurions to a council-of-war, at which he harangued them mercilessly, and announced that, instead of waiting any longer, he was breaking camp during the final watch of the night. ' "And if no-one else follows me," he added, "I shall march with the Tenth Legion alone. I have not the slightest doubt about their loyalty, and they shall be my personal escort as commander" ' (*The Gallic War* I. 40).

Seven days later, Caesar's scouts reported that Ariovistus was not much more than a day's march away. This time, it was Ariovistus who opened the diplomatic proceedings. He announced that he would meet Caesar, but on condition that each party should be escorted only by cavalry. Caesar, who did not trust his Gallic auxiliary cavalry any more than he did Ariovistus, borrowed some cavalry horses and mounted on them soldiers from the Tenth Legion. This prompted one of them to observe that Caesar was now conferring on them 'equestrian' rank. The term stuck, and from then until it was reformed and renamed, the legion was known as the Tenth *Equestris*.

The principals duly met, but in the middle of a long parley Caesar broke off negotiations when it was reported to him that some German cavalry were throwing missiles and stones at his escort. Two days later, Ariovistus offered to renew the talks, to which Caesar could, if he wished, send an intermediary. Caesar, not wanting to risk the lives of any of his personal staff, nominated Gaius Valerius Procillus, a high-born native of the province of Transalpine Gaul whose father had been awarded Roman citizenship, and another Gaul who was known personally to Ariovistus. When Ariovistus saw them, he accused them of being spies and had them thrown into chains.

Caesar, not very reluctantly, was being forced to give battle. For six days, the two sides fenced and skirmished. Then Caesar learned from prisoners the reason why Ariovistus was drawing out the proceedings. It was customary, before a battle, for German prophetesses to divine whether or not the omens were favourable by taking lots, represented by pieces of wood carrying mystical signs. The verdict had been that there would be no victory for Ariovistus before the new moon, which would occur on 20 September. On 18 September, Caesar advanced towards the German camp with his six legions, drawn up in three lines. Ariovistus had no choice but to respond, deploying his army in front of his wagons, from which the women and children of the tribe could watch the fighting and give vocal support.

Both sides charged at each other so fiercely that there was no time for the Romans to hurl their javelins. They ran in with their swords, some even leaping onto the German shield wall and thrusting down from above. Caesar's right wing, under his personal command, shattered the German left. The Roman left wing, however, was in trouble, but young Publius Crassus, in charge of the auxiliary cavalry waiting in the rear, saw what was happening and, on his own initiative, rode forward and ordered the third line of the Roman right wing to disengage and reinforce their comrades on the left. Victory became a rout. Some of the Germans who escaped managed to swim the Rhine to safety; the rest were pursued and slaughtered. Ariovistus got across in a boat, but both of his wives and one of his two daughters were killed as they fled. Caesar, riding now with the cavalry, personally rescued Procillus, who had three times been saved from being burned alive by the lots being in his favour.

The Suebi who had been massing on the east bank of the Rhine, waiting for the signal to cross and invade Gaul, thought better of it, and went home. Caesar, triumphant after two campaigns brilliantly won in quick time, gave his army the rest of the season off. Labienus was given command and put in charge of supervising the construction of winter quarters in the territory of the Sequani. Caesar retired to Cisalpine Gaul, ostensibly to attend to the administration of justice throughout the province on a peripatetic basis, but more probably to consider the implications of what had in the meantime been happening in Rome, where Clodius had been continuing to give notice of the havoc one man could cause to the constitution.

The most important man in Rome was undeniably Pompey, and for this reason he was resented by the senate. Clodius seems to have decided that by using his position to attack Pompey, he would lose nothing in popular esteem, but might earn some kudos with the senate. It was an unusual, and devastating, political campaign. He began by undermining Pompey's standing as the authority on eastern affairs with a bill to replace Deiotarus, tetrarch of Galatia, Pompey's nominee as high priest in the cult of the Great Goddess (Cybele) in Pessinus, with Brogitarus, Deiotarus's son-in-law, who had almost certainly bribed Clodius to do so.

Clodius then devised an even more audacious stratagem to humiliate Pompey. After defeating Mithridates, Pompey had allowed Tigranes, who was son-in-law to Mithridates, to retain his kingdom of Armenia, and had brought back to Rome as a hostage Tigranes's son, also called Tigranes. Tigranes *fils* was kept under house arrest in the home of Lucius Flavius, who was a praetor in that year of 58 BC. Clodius, while dining one day as a guest in Flavius's house, asked if he could see Tigranes, and invited him to join them at the table. He then walked out of the house, taking Tigranes with him. When Flavius protested, Clodius reminded him that as a tribune, his person was inviolable. Even Pompey was refused access to Tigranes, whom Clodius now put on a ship to return him to Armenia. The ship was wrecked off Antium shortly after the start of its voyage, and its passengers were put ashore. Clodius sent his clerk, Sextus Cloelius, to fetch Tigranes. On the Appian Way, Cloelius and his escort clashed with Flavius and his guards, who were bent on the same mission. There was bloodshed, and one of Pompey's associates was killed.

Something had to be done about the maverick Clodius. In a remarkable incident probably instigated by Pompey, the consul Aulus Gabinius tried to match force with force in the streets. The consul's heavies were ousted by Clodius's thugs, and the *fasces* were broken in pieces. It was time once again for diplomacy. In a move which was bound to be vetoed but which demonstrated the solidarity of the senate, its members voted unanimously in favour of a proposal to bring back Cicero from banishment. Clodius responded by instigating measures, backed by Bibulus and some members of the pontifical college, to declare improper on religious grounds all Caesar's acts as consul, except the bill allowing Clodius to become a plebeian. Somehow these fell by the wayside, so Clodius resorted to violent tactics again.

Immediately after the consular elections for 57 BC, one of Clodius's slaves was seen to drop a dagger as Pompey walked by to go to a meeting of the senate. When the slave was apprehended and questioned, he replied, as he had been coached to do, that he had been instructed to assassinate Pompey. At this, Pompey, in an uncharacteristic demonstration of spinelessness, shut himself up in his house for the rest of the year, regularly taunted by Clodius's street gangs, who took to besieging the place. A further bill was now promulgated, this time by eight of the tribunes of 58 BC, calling for Cicero's return. It was duly vetoed, but the point had been made, and one of the tribunes-elect travelled north to consult Caesar on the matter of Cicero. Caesar was sublimely non-committal. In the end official permission for Cicero's return to Rome was not given until August 57 BC, after Caesar had backed the measure once he realized that it was inevitable. Meanwhile, he had military considerations on his mind.

The presence of six legions wintering in the very heart of Gaul was especially unnerving to the predominantly Germanic tribes to the north, some of which formed a coalition, under the leadership of the Belgae, to oppose Rome. Caesar responded by opening the season of 57 BC at the head of two new legions (Thirteenth and Fourteenth) which he had raised in Cisalpine Gaul. At the end of protracted skirmishing in the vicinity of the river Somme, the Belgic coalition remained as threatening as ever, but two of the northern tribes, the Bellovaci and the Remi, had submitted to Rome and provided hostages. The stage was set for another major confrontation. When it came, at the river Sambre, Caesar was caught napping.

Three tribes, the Atrebates, Nervii, and Viromandui, had established themselves on flat, wooded ground sloping down to the south bank of the river. The Romans, having reconnoitred a suitable site for their camp on the opposite bank, began to bring their troops up from the position at which they had halted some 10 miles away to the north. The tribes were expecting the Roman line of march to comprise each legion marching *sub sarcinis* (that is, with every man carrying his personal kit, weapons, and trenching tools), followed by its own baggage train, and thus that there would be ample time and opportunity to pick off the leading legions as they arrived. Caesar's tactics, however, because he was in the vicinity of an enemy, were to send his six experienced legions ahead *expediti* (in light marching order, carrying little else but their arms), followed by the whole baggage train, with the Thirteenth and Fourteenth legions protecting it in the rear.

Even so, the six leading legions had only just arrived on the scene, and the baggage train and its guard were still strung out across country, when the Belgic tribes came out of their protective woods, crossed the river in force, and attacked. There was no time to form ranks. Each man simply rallied to the nearest standard. The Ninth and Tenth legions, who were on the left of the line, stood firm, and then drove the opposition back across the river with great slaughter. The Nervii, however, pushed back the Roman right, and were threatening to encircle it when Caesar arrived from supervising the troops on the left of the haphazard line. He seized a shield from a legionary in one of the rear ranks, and dashed to the front. There he ran up and down, steadying the ranks, and personally encouraging individual centurions by name.

The day was saved by the arrival of the two legions who had been bringing up the rear of the march, and by the ubiquitous Tenth, whom Labienus ordered to disengage and join battle on the Roman right. The fighting complement of the Nervii was wiped out. The older men of the tribe, hiding in the countryside with the women and children, surrendered to Caesar, who told them to go back to their homes and gave orders that neighbouring tribes were not to molest them.

He was less generous to the Aduatuci. Their warriors had been on their way to back up the Nervii when they heard of the disaster at the Sambre. They returned home and, with their families and chattels, fortified themselves in their hill-top stronghold. Caesar invested the whole town with a fortified rampart, two and three-quarter miles long, with forts set at close intervals. Then, under protective covering, a ramp and a siege tower were built some distance from the town. The Aduatuci on the wall hooted with laughter that such a great engine of war should be built so far away, until they saw it trundling towards them on wheels. Caesar then offered to spare their lives if they would give up all their arms. This they appeared to do, throwing them down from the top of the wall. It was only, however, a partial decommissioning. That night, several thousand armed Aduatuci broke out of the town and attacked the Roman camp. Most of them were killed; the rest retreated back through the town gates. The next morning the Romans forced their way in. Caesar laconically describes the fate of the inmates: 'Caesar sold off the whole town, lock, stock, and barrel. The dealers gave him a receipt for 53,000 head of people' (*The Gallic War* II. 33). Slave dealers accompanied armies in the ancient world, hoping to pick up their merchandise cheaply and in bulk. Sometimes, however, they got things spectacularly wrong, as they did in 165 BC, when they backed the Syrians to defeat the Maccabaean Jews.

Meanwhile, Publius Crassus, who had been despatched with the Seventh Legion to subdue the Veneti and other northern maritime tribes, reported that his mission had been accomplished. Caesar disposed his legions for the winter near various potential trouble spots, and left for Illyricum, having informed the senate that there was now peace throughout Gaul. The senate announced 15 days of thanksgiving in his name, an honour never before granted to anyone, even Pompey.

Then Caesar's private world of ambitious plans and hopes for the future began to fall apart. Cicero was home, and in full voice in the senate. He was particularly venomous about Aulus Gabinius and Calpurnius Piso, whom he held responsible for his exile; in among the personal insults was enough plausible evidence of wrongdoing to persuade the senate to recall Piso from his post in 55 BC, though Piso vigorously and successfully defended himself against the charges. Pompey too had returned to public life, having decided that the only way to neutralize Clodius, who was still causing endless trouble as an ordinary citizen, was to mobilize his own private army of urban guerrillas, under a leader capable of beating Clodius at his own game. This was Titus Annius Milo, elected a tribune for 57, who was of good family, capable, and wealthy (and thus popular for his provision of public entertainments). He was also a friend of Cicero.

Pompey was looking for a post with *imperium* which would enable him to steal some of Caesar's military thunder. Clodius had unwittingly provided the basis; Cicero supplied the means. Clodius's corn measures had caused the system of supply to collapse. There were problems of production, price, and distribution, culminating in a riot. Cicero proposed, and the consuls drafted a bill accordingly, that Pompey should be appointed corn supremo for five years, to administer the basic food supply throughout the empire, with 15 deputies to assist him. This was a roving commission, centred on Rome, which enabled Pompey to exercise, in terms of the Roman world, global influence.

Caesar's grip on the ebb and flow of government was also being prised away. In December 57 BC Publius Rutilius Rufus, recently elected tribune, started to unpick Caesar's second land law. Caesar's man Publius Vatinius was beaten in the elections for aedile, postponed until January 56 BC. Lucius

Domitius Ahenobarbus gave notice that he would stand at the next consular elections, and if successful would remove Caesar from his command. And Cato would then be back to support the motion.

Caesar, having finished his business in Illyricum in the autumn of 57 BC, made the rounds of Cisalpine Gaul. It was not unknown for a wife to be with her husband during his assignment as provincial governor, unless he was on campaign. Thus it is possible that Calpurnia was in Cisalpine Gaul during times when he was engaged in administrative duties. He was, however, a restless person, never content to stay long in one place, and he was in Ravenna in March 56 BC, when he received a visitor – Crassus. On 7 April, Cicero in Rome called on Pompey, who was due shortly to leave for Sardinia to organize corn supplies. On 8 April, Cicero wrote to his brother Quintus, who was already in Sardinia as one of the corn supremo's deputies, saying that Pompey was on his way but had not yet decided whether to sail from Pisa or another port.

Pompey was bluffing about his movements. A few days later, he had a secret summit meeting with Caesar and Crassus at Luca, a few miles from Pisa. The effrontery of their plans effectively to divide between themselves the government of the empire was breathtaking. Crassus and Pompey would arrange that they, and not Ahenobarbus and a colleague, would be consuls in 55 BC. While in power they would secure a five-year extension of Caesar's present provincial commands, without any break between one term and the next during which he might face prosecution. Crassus and Pompey would also organize for themselves plum five-year postings as provincial governors after their spell as consuls.

There had been trouble during the winter in north-western Gaul, where the maritime tribes, at the instigation of the Veneti, had come to an agreement among themselves to imprison the supplies' officers that Publius Crassus had sent to commandeer corn, until their own hostages were returned. Caesar's response was to mount an elaborate campaign on five fronts, designed to root out the problem and prevent it spreading to other parts of Gaul. To fight the Veneti, who were a sea-going nation, he had a fleet built on the river Loire, drafted in crews from Transalpine Gaul, and put Decimus Brutus in charge of operations.

The sea victory over the Veneti, whose ships were taller and more man-oeuvrable in shallow waters, was a triumph for Roman ingenuity rather than Roman seamanship. The Venetian ships depended entirely on sails and carried no archers on board. The Romans were able to row right up to them and attach sharp hooks mounted on poles to the rigging supporting the yardarms and sails. When the Romans rowed away at full speed, the ropes tautened and snapped, causing the yardarms and sails to collapse in heaps on the deck. Seeing this, the rest of the Venetian fleet sailed away to safety, only to be caught in a sudden calm. They were picked off one by one, in the course of a series of battles lasting eight hours, during which the infantry that manned the Roman ships proved superior to the fighting men in the Venetian vessels.

The Veneti, having lost their ships, their fighting men, and alongside them many of their leaders, surrendered as a tribe. Caesar, claiming as justification that his corn supplies' officers had diplomatic status, made an example of them: he had the whole Venetian ruling council executed, and sold the rest of the population to the slave dealers.

There was a somewhat frustrating end-of-season campaign against the Morini, who still refused to submit to Rome and, after Caesar had marched his troops 400 miles to make them see the error of their ways, simply disappeared into the forests. He then returned to Cisalpine Gaul, no doubt to savour the news that was coming in from Rome.

Crassus and Pompey achieved their election by shameless manipulation of the system. When one of the consuls for 56 BC, Gnaeus Cornelius Lentulus Marcellinus, refused to allow them to stand on the grounds that they had not given sufficient notice of their intention, they bribed a tribune, Gaius Cato, to hold up all elections for the year by announcing that the omens were unfavourable. Elections for the consuls for 55 BC were therefore held during an interregnum in January of that year. As a result of intimidation, there were only three candidates: Crassus, Pompey, and Ahenobarbus, who was energetically supported by his brother-in-law, Cato. The position of Ahenobarbus became hopeless, however, when Publius Crassus brought home on leave 1000 of Caesar's men to swell the ranks of the eligible electorate – there was no doubt for whom they would vote.

The night before the elections, however, Ahenobarbus ventured out with a small group of supporters, hoping to pick up a few votes. His torch bearer was attacked and killed, Cato was wounded, and he himself had to flee for his life back to his house. The next day, Crassus and Pompey were elected consuls.

Their first task was to arrange the elections of senior state officials to suit themselves, in the course of which, while voting was actually taking place, Pompey blocked Cato's path to a praetorship by declaring the election null and void on the grounds that he had heard thunder. Then by extensive bribery, and not a little intimidation, he and Crassus secured the election of Publius Vatinius in his place. Shortly after this, the tribune Gaius Trebonius proposed the utterly unconstitutional motion that at the end of their year of office Crassus should be granted the province of Syria and Pompey both parts of Spain for a period of five years, with full authority to raise troops and to make war or peace with whomever they wished. There was opposition, predictably from Cato, less predictably from two of the tribunes, who were only given by Trebonius limited time to speak against his motion. Voting took place, and the bill became law, as had become customary in an atmosphere of intimidation and violence. According to Cassius Dio, Crassus and Pompey were eye-witnesses to these disturbances, and immediately called another vote on the extension of Caesar's command for a further five years. This too was passed.

During the election that year for aediles, there occurred a distressing family incident. On election day itself, there were violent clashes between rival supporters, many of whom were killed. Pompey, who appears to have been personally involved, had his clothes splashed with blood. It seems that he took off his toga and told some of his slaves to take it back to the house, presumably to get Julia to replace it with a clean one. Julia, who was pregnant, took one look at it and fainted away, suffering a miscarriage in the process. The details are recorded by Plutarch, who goes out of his way also to stress how much Pompey loved his wife, and she him.

Crassus, who saw his appointment to Syria as an excuse to enrich himself further and also to earn military laurels by starting a war with the Parthians, left Rome with his entourage and army in November 55 BC. Pompey too had been enlisting troops, but he seemed in no hurry to leave for Spain. Apart from anything else, he was basking in the public glory he had earned from the dedication in August of his theatre on the Campus Martius. This sporting, entertainment, and conference complex was built with the personal profits from his exploits in the east. It incorporated a temple, a theatre for dramatic and musical performances, an amphitheatre for games and gladiatorial shows, a hall sufficiently large and well appointed to accommodate meetings of the senate, and pleasure gardens.

Caesar had made an early start to the campaign of 55 BC. The trouble-makers this time were two northern Germanic tribes, the Usipetes and Tencteri, who had been displaced by the restless Suebi and were looking for new homelands west of the Rhine. Caesar's intelligence services had informed him that certain Gallic tribes had already offered them hospitality. To him, this was a serious challenge to his authority and a dangerous precedent should other Germanic tribes, similarly pressed for *lebensraum*, follow their example. Having no regular mounted troops, he called a meeting of Gallic chiefs, whom he no longer trusted, and requisitioned 5000 auxiliary cavalry. His march took him to, and possibly across, the river Meuse. Protracted negotiations now ensued between the two sides, both of whom were guilty of sharp practice. Caesar's cavalry, advancing under a banner of truce, were set upon and put to flight by 800 German horse, losing 74 men. The next day, a large contingent of Germans, including all their senior officers, came to Caesar's camp to apologize for the behaviour of their horsemen and to gain more time for the main body of their cavalry to return from an expedition (of which Caesar was well aware) to raise loot and corn, by asking for the truce to be extended. Caesar, having got the Germans precisely where he wanted, gleefully had the whole mission detained; then he led out his entire army in battle formation, with the suspect and demoralized cavalry in the rear.

He covered the eight miles to the German camp before anyone there was aware of what was happening.

Everything contributed to their sudden panic; the speed of our arrival, the absence of their commanders, the lack of time to pick up their arms, let alone to think what to do, left them utterly at a loss to decide what was best – attack the enemy in force, defend the camp, or seek refuge in flight. When their fear became evident from the cries and confusion, our men, stirred up by the treachery of the previous day, burst into the camp. There, those who were able to take up their arms quickly resisted for a short time, fighting among the carts and baggage-wagons. The rest, consisting of a crowd of women and children (for the tribes had left their homes and crossed the Rhine with all their belongings), started to flee in all directions; Caesar sent his cavalry after them.

*The Gallic War* IV. 14

There was carnage, too, at the river, where survivors were cut down or threw themselves into the water, and drowned. Not a Roman life was lost.

This was clearly a massacre. Caesar was not given to wanton brutality. When he did display a cruel side, it was because he saw positive political benefits in his doing so. Usually this was to make a point to others who might be considering a similar course of action, in this case the Germanic tribes to the east of the Rhine and the Gauls who might assist them. Ancient attitudes to brutality were different from those of today. Even so, though some of his friends in Rome proposed that there should be a public thanks-giving for his victory, a senatorial enquiry was set up to look into the treat-ment of the peoples of Gaul, and Cato proposed in the senate that Caesar not only should apologize to the Germans but should be handed over to those whom he had treated so outrageously.

Caesar, however, had not finished yet. As a final show of force, he decided to cross the Rhine into enemy territory. He refused the offer of friendly tribesmen to ferry his army to the other side in boats, as being beneath his dignity. The Rhine at Coblenz is 400 metres wide, and 6 to 8 metres deep. Caesar's engineers constructed a timber bridge right the way across, carrying a roadway 11 metres wide. The weight was borne by massive piles, 44 cm in diameter, driven into the stony river bed at an angle, so that the powerful current would not disturb them. Transverse beams, 59 cm thick, supported poles laid lengthwise and surfaced with wattlework. According to Caesar himself, it was finished in 10 days, which a BBC research team has concluded, given the human skills and natural resources available to him, was quite feasible. He now took his army across into German territory where, for 18 days, his men burned villages and buildings, and cut down and des-troyed crops. Then he returned across the bridge which, having served its purpose, was broken up.

For some time it had been part of his grand design to add the mysterious island of Britain to his list of conquests. To crown the year, before taking his winter recess in Italy, he would take an expeditionary force of two legions into the unknown. Caesar himself claimed that the Celts in Britain had been supporting the Celts on the mainland and needed teaching a lesson. Suetonius said he was after pearls, which, if this observation is true, must have proved a disappointment, as British pearls were of poor quality. Nor was there much of value to be obtained by way of booty, except slaves, and these, according to Cicero, were at the lower end of the market since they had no musical or secretarial skills. It is as likely that Caesar feared being recalled the following year by a senate which might regard him as having achieved his objectives in Gaul. And a successful high-profile campaign would do him no harm in his rivalry with Pompey for public acclaim and support.

Before embarking, he sent an officer to spy out the land and report back, but the man dared not leave his ship for fear of what might happen to him in the hands of the barbarians – the Romans regarded everyone as a barbarian who lived outside the frontiers of the Roman empire. Word had come, however, through traders that various of the Celtic tribes in Britain were not averse to accepting the rule of Rome. To them he sent as his ambassador Commius, whom he had in 57 BC made king of the Gallic Atrebates, an offshoot of which tribe occupied lands in Britain south of the river Thames. On his arrival in Britain, though, Commius was seized and put in chains, but later released.

Caesar embarked the Seventh and Tenth legions at Boulogne in 80 transports which he had commandeered from local tribes and set sail during the night of 25 August 55 BC. He ordered a further 18 transports, which could not make the rendezvous because of the wind, to pick up 500 cavalry a few miles to the north. When his flagship reached the coast of Britain, he sailed eastwards, looking for somewhere to land, while on shore tribesmen tracked the fleet, hurling missiles and abuse from the cliffs. He finally decided to disembark his army on the shore by Deal, but because it was low tide his ships could not get in close enough. Instead his soldiers had to drop down into the water and wade to the beach, carrying their personal kit and arms, in the face of a concentration of enemy missiles and cavalry assaults.

By using his ships' longboats and his reconnaissance vessels to ferry troops in to support the men who were struggling ashore, Caesar managed to conjure victory out of chaos. Without his cavalry, which owing to the weather never arrived at all, he could not follow up this initial success, nor properly combat the fast Celtic chariots, each manned by a driver and a warrior. He did, however, arrive in the nick of time from his base camp to prevent the Seventh Legion, who had been sent out into the fields to forage for corn, being ambushed and annihilated.

Caesar was lucky to get his troops back across the Channel at all. He totally misjudged the tides and the weather, and as a result the ships which he had drawn up on the shore were flooded, and the transports lying out at anchor were subjected to such fierce gales that several of them broke up and others were too damaged to sail. He crammed his soldiers into the ships which had survived, and withdrew for the winter. He brought with him only a few of the Celtic hostages he had demanded, telling the rest to report to him in Gaul. Only a handful ever turned up.

Before leaving for Italy, he ordered a new invasion fleet of 28 galleys and 600 transports to be built to his specifications. The latter would be broader and of a shallower draught than usual, for ease of beaching and unloading, and would be equipped with oars as well as sails. He had thus signalled his intention to return to Britain the following year.

It had been an inglorious exploit. The senate, however, on receipt of Caesar's dispatches, ordered 20 days of public thanksgiving for his achievements.

Octavia

# 6

# THE GENERAL
## Britain to the Rubicon 54–49 BC

> In less than 10 years in Gaul, Caesar successfully stormed over
> 800 cities, subdued 300 tribes, and fought hand-to-hand bat-
> tles against a total of three million warriors, of whom he killed
> a million, and took as many more prisoner.
>
> Plutarch, *Caesar* 15

During that winter, Caesar had to suffer a personal indignity of a different
kind. His relations with his chief engineer in Gaul, Mamurra, were the
subject of some scurrilous verses by the poet Gaius Valerius Catullus, at one
time a lover of Publius Clodius's sister:

> A fine couple of shameless sodomites,
>     Mamurra and sex-mad Caesar . . .
> Perverted bedmates,
>     They compete against each other
> At serial adultery and
>     Pulling teenage birds.
>                 Catullus LVII. 1–10

Catullus's father, a leading citizen of Verona at whose house Caesar often used to stay when wintering in his province, was so appalled at his son's indiscretion that he ordered him personally to apologize. Caesar, who had a forgiving nature when it suited him, admitted that he found the verses extremely offensive, but accepted the apology and invited Catullus to dine with him later that day. He also remained on friendly terms with the young man's father.

When the year of 54 BC began, Pompey broke with precedent by remaining in Italy instead of travelling to take up his commission in Spain, which he deputed to his legates, Lucius Afranius, his long-term associate who had been consul in 60 BC, and Marcus Petreius, veteran soldier and supporter of Cato. He used his responsibility for the corn supply as a justification. As a provincial governor, he could not enter the city of Rome, but he hovered near enough to be able personally to influence matters at a time when Lucius Domitius Ahenobarbus had now succeeded in gaining the consulship and Cato had been elected a praetor.

Caesar's response was to court popularity, and counter Pompey's architectural triumph, by spending vast amounts from the booty he had taken in Gaul on lavish building projects. There would be an extension to the forum, for which the site alone cost him, according to Suetonius, 100 million sesterces. Construction began immediately on the Basilica Julia, a three-storey building, 101 metres long and 49 metres wide, for official gatherings and markets. In addition, Cicero noted, 'We are to have a roofed-in enclosure made of marble for meetings of the tribal assembly, surrounded by a high colonnade a mile long' (*To Atticus* IV. 17).

On the political front, Caesar strengthened his team of correspondents by maintaining regular contact with Cicero, to whom he lent the considerable sum of 800,000 sesterces – three years later it had not yet been paid back. The letters between them have not survived, or were never published, but the relationship between two men of towering intellect and considerable literary pretensions, neither of whom fully trusted the other, seems to have been marked by banter and pleasant courtesies. *De Analogia*, Caesar's treatise on grammar, which he dictated in the spring of 54 BC on his journey to Gaul, was dedicated to Cicero. Over the next few years Caesar compiled an anthology of Cicero's jokes and sayings, which was published in 46 BC. Cicero returned the compliment by writing an epic poem on Caesar's expedition to Britain, having earlier submitted to Caesar for an opinion a narrative poem describing his own exile and return. Of the opening book, Caesar said that he had read nothing better even in Greek literature; the latter parts, however, he thought a bit careless. Cicero was somewhat put out to receive anything but effusive praise, and asked his brother Quintus for some elucidation, adding that of course this made no difference whatsoever to what he thought about his own work.

In Gaul, trouble blew up while Caesar was waiting for the fleet to be ready at Boulogne. The influential Treveri, who never attended Caesar's council meetings of tribal representatives, now refused to supply him with troops, and were revealed to be in discussion with Germanic tribes east of the Rhine. Caesar took four legions, marching light, and 800 cavalry into their territory, which was enough for diplomatic advances to be made to him. There were two opposing factions within the tribe, led respectively by Cingetorix and Indutiomarus. Cingetorix took the initiative by pledging his loyalties to Rome. Caesar then rebuffed overtures of friendship from Indutiomarus, and ordered him to hand over 200 hostages, including his son and the rest of his family.

Then he returned to Boulogne, where he had ordered all the tribal chiefs of Gaul, with 4000 Celtic cavalry for his use, to assemble. Of those that arrived, he immediately detained any that he thought might be antagonistic to Rome, to be kept under his personal supervision on the expedition to Britain, so that they could not make trouble in his absence. Dumnorix of the Aedui pleaded to be excused on the grounds that he was a bad sailor. When Caesar refused to release him, he stirred up dissent among the chiefs. Finally, as the troops were beginning to embark after a north-west wind had caused a delay of 25 days, Dumnorix escaped with a troop of Aeduan cavalry. The sailing was cancelled, and Dumnorix was hunted down and killed; his horsemen returned to Caesar.

The vast invasion fleet of, according to Caesar, over 800 ships, including private vessels owned or hired by traders expecting pickings from the campaign, sailed at about 9 p.m. on 6 July 54 BC. The landing on the beaches near Deal was unopposed. To save time, Caesar anchored the ships that would remain with him off the unprotected shore, rather than drag them up on the beach. The rest he sent back empty to Gaul, before marching inland by night to find the opposition – surprise and speed were his tactical trademarks. He was organizing a mopping up operation after a successful encounter near Bigbury, when he was told that his fleet had been wrecked again. The damage was catastrophic. Some ships had dragged their anchors in the storm or snapped their cables, and had been bodily thrown up on the beach. Others had crashed against each other in the water and broken up. Caesar returned to the scene of destruction and ordered those ships which were not damaged beyond repair to be rebuilt. To enable this to be done, he withdrew craftsmen from his legions and obtained ships' carpenters from Gaul. He also wrote to Labienus that as many ships as possible should be constructed by the army in Gaul. Then, having had the ships that were to be repaired drawn up on the beach within an entrenched and palisaded extension to the camp, he started out again after the native British Celts.

The Britons were waiting for him. As leader, they had elected Cassivellaunus, from north of the Thames. For a time his guerrilla tactics succeeded, but it was inevitable that he would make a stand somewhere. On the first occasion, south of the Thames, Caesar's three legions, with supporting cavalry, caused the Britons to retreat. Cassivellaunus, having somehow got several thousand of his chariots back across the Thames, took up a position on the far bank, where there was a ford, which he fortified above and below the water-line with sharpened stakes pointing outwards. Caesar sent his cavalry across first, followed by the legions up to their necks in the water. So fierce was the assault that the Britons abandoned their stations and retreated into the woods, from which Cassivellaunus was able to shadow, with his remaining chariots, the progress of the army, and move people and cattle out of the way of its march.

Caesar now received practical support from Mandubracius of the powerful Trinovantes, whose father had been killed by Cassivellaunus. His envoys offered Caesar the tribe's surrender in return for protection from Cassivellaunus and the recognition by Rome of the right of Mandubracius to rule the Trinovantes. Caesar demanded in return 40 hostages and corn for his whole army, which temporarily resolved his ongoing food supply problem. Other tribes in the vicinity followed suit, and with their help Caesar was able to find Cassivellaunus's stronghold, which he took with a double-pronged attack. Cassivellaunus's attempt to delay the inevitable, by persuading the maritime tribes in Kent to make a concerted attack on the Roman naval camp, failed against the garrison of 10 cohorts and 300 cavalry which Caesar had left there to guard the ships.

Cassivellaunus, who was no fool, capitulated rather than endure a long war of attrition. Caesar's negotiator was Commius. Britain had, however, been given a lengthy breathing space of 97 years before the Roman legions would return in force. Caesar, in the course of two campaigns, had achieved nothing tangible. He was, however, anxious to return to Gaul for the winter, having had reports there of 'unexpected disturbances' (*The Gallic War* V. 22). He fixed an annual rate of tribute from the British tribes, of which probably only the first instalment was paid, and requisitioned a large number of hostages and prisoners.

He still, however, had to get his troops back to Gaul before the autumn equinox. The refurbished ships were lying ready, but even with the 60 new ships which Labienus had built, and the original ones which had returned to Gaul, it would still be necessary to make two trips. In the end, because of the weather, only a few of the ships from Gaul reached Britain; the rest were driven back by the wind and tides. Caesar packed his transports tighter than he had intended, and brought his army and his human booty safely across at one time. He had at least proved that it was possible to invade Britain, and it was through him that links were established with tribes there who were friendly to, or sufficiently frightened of, Rome. Whatever his motives may have been, without his initiative it is unlikely that Britain, for better or for worse, would ever have been part of the Roman empire.

It was when Caesar got back to Gaul, according to Plutarch, that he received the news, in letters from friends, that Julia had died in childbirth, and that the baby survived for only a few days. Pompey had lost a beloved young wife, and Caesar his only child from three marriages. It was Caesar's second personal tragedy in one year, the other being the death of his mother, Aurelia. It is not clear how far Julia's death was the cause, or the beginning, of any breakdown in relations between the two pre-eminent men in the Roman world, especially as Suetonius records that until the outbreak of the civil war Caesar retained Pompey as his principal legatee, and used to read out that part of his will to his assembled troops. What is certain, however, is that Julia, had she lived, would have been a calming influence on, and a potential mediator between, the two most significant men in her life, each of whom resented the other's reputation.

Suetonius is also the source of an offer Caesar now made to his former son-in-law. Pompey should marry Caesar's great-niece Octavia, who was married to Gaius Claudius Marcellus. Caesar himself would divorce Calpurnia, and instead marry Pompey's daughter with Mucia, Pompeia, the wife of Sulla's son, Faustus Cornelius Sulla. Pompey would have none of it, so all deals were off, and everyone remained married to their present partners. As marriage in Rome was based on consent, all that was required for divorce was the consent of either party, or of the wife's father. Cato was at about this time involved in a bizarre instance. He was invited by the orator Hortensius to dissolve his daughter Porcia's marriage to Marcus Bibulus so that Hortensius could marry her himself. Cato refused. Hortensius then persuaded Cato to divorce his own wife, Marcia, whom Hortensius now married. When Hortensius died in 49 BC at the age of 65, leaving Marcia a rich widow, Cato remarried her.

Meanwhile Crassus had been energetically enriching himself in Syria. He denuded the great Temple in Jerusalem of its treasures, and then in 53 BC embarked on his misguided attempt to acquire military laurels by taking on the Parthians. There was a grim prelude to the main conflict, which took place near Carrhae. Publius Crassus had brought from Gaul 1000 cavalry to bolster his father's army. Seeing what appeared to be small detachments of Parthians, he led out his cavalry squadron against them, only to be caught out by a traditional Parthian strategem. The Parthians retreated; Publius followed them. Then more of the enemy appeared from behind hillocks and woody areas. He and his horsemen were cut off from the main army, and butchered. Publius could have escaped, but instead he committed suicide. The Parthians cut off his head and stuck it on a spear, which they carried up and down in front of the Roman lines where Crassus could see it. In the ensuing battle, Crassus was ignominiously defeated, and was then murdered while attempting to negotiate the terms of his surrender. It is said that his head was cut off, and molten gold poured into his mouth, as a symbol of his greed.

Matters in Rome were becoming far too chaotic for there to be much heart searching over the defeat; because of accusations of corruption and of other scandalous practices, the consular elections for 53 BC did not take place until the summer of that year. Pompey, however, now took the opportunity to marry, as his fifth wife, the widow of Publius Crassus, Cornelia, who was probably young enough to be his granddaughter. She was of the clan Metellus, her father, Quintus Caecilius Metellus Pius Scipio, being an adopted son of Quintus Metellus Pius. The confusion over elections, however, did not deter those seeking offices for 52 BC from actively campaigning. Among them were Milo for consul and Clodius for praetor.

The 'unexpected disturbances' which had required Caesar's attention in Gaul exploded into a bloodbath. A poor harvest in 54 BC forced Caesar to dispose his troops in winter quarters over a wider area than was his custom. Ambiorix, chief of the Eburones, took advantage of this. While professing friendship to Rome, he inveigled the Fourteenth Legion at Aduatuca into abandoning its camp for reasons of safety, to join up with the legion in the territory of the Nervii, which was commanded by Quintus Cicero, brother of Cicero. The column was ambushed and massacred on the way.

Ambiorix now personally encouraged the Nervii to besiege Quintus Cicero, which they did so enthusiastically and successfully that Cicero was forced to ask for Caesar's help. Caesar was at Amiens. With two legions, one less than he would have liked, he left immediately. The Nervii broke off the siege and surged along the way to meet him. In sight of the enemy, Caesar, out-numbered by ten to one, deliberately constructed an overnight camp smaller than would normally be the case, in order to confuse the opposition as to his numbers. Then he ordered his men to feign panic. The Nervii, scenting an easy victory, were gathering for the kill when a concerted sally, from all the camp gates at once, put them to flight. Caesar was only just in time. When Cicero's men were paraded for him, nine-tenths of them were walking wounded.

Early in 53 BC, before the winter was over, Caesar collected four legions and descended on the Nervii so suddenly that they had no time to mobilize any opposition. He took numerous people and cattle as booty, and distrib-uted them to his troops. Then he called for the Nervii formally to surrender

*Figure 6.1* Silver *denarius* of 49 BC, the first coin to be associated with Caesar. It shows (obverse) an elephant trampling on a snake, representing Gaul, and (reverse) implements associated with the priesthood, including the cap that features in figure 3.1. (× 2)

to him again, and demanded hostages. The tribe was lucky in a way. For Caesar, on hearing of the massacre of the legion from Aduatuca, had vowed neither to shave nor have his hair cut until its men had been properly avenged.

While various groupings of hostile tribes were taking place, Caesar raised two new legions, the Fourteenth and Fifteenth, and borrowed another from Pompey. The new Fourteenth, which replaced the legion which had been destroyed, was put under the command of Quintus Cicero and set to guard the army's main baggage camp at Aduatuca, where the wounded were being cared for. During the year Caesar held conferences of Gallic chiefs, and took punitive action against those who failed to turn up. He neatly avoided committing his legionaries to fighting the Eburones in the unfavourable forests by inviting neighbouring tribes to help him pillage their lands. The news spread across the Rhine, where the Sugambri raised 2000 horsemen and crossed the river on boats and rafts to join in the fun. Having helped themselves to what pickings had been left, they were informed by a prisoner that the Roman baggage camp was only three hours away. The Sugambri melted away in the direction of Aduatuca.

There developed at Aduatuca a tremendous battle, in which the Roman sick took their places beside their fitter, but less experienced, colleagues. Eventually the Germans retired, but rumours spread through the camp that they would not have attacked in the first place unless Caesar with his legions had been defeated. These were dispelled by the arrival of Caesar himself, who afterwards commented wryly that, 'Of all these incidents, the most remarkable seemed to be that the Germans, who had crossed the Rhine with the express intention of ravaging the lands of Ambiorix, by bearing down on the Roman camp did him the greatest service' (*The Gallic War* VI. 42). The truth was that Ambiorix had escaped from the devastation; no-one knew, or ever discovered, where he was. Caesar, however, took his revenge out on Acco, chief of the Senones, who had incited his tribe not to co-operate with the Romans. At the next meeting of the chiefs, he was flogged to death.

'Now that Gaul was quiet' (*The Gallic War* VII. 1), Caesar, as was his custom, wintered in Cisalpine Gaul, observing from a distance events in Rome, where the year's first market day, held every ninth day, fell in 52 BC on 1 January. This, to superstitious Romans, was not so much a happy coincidence as a portent of disaster. Subsequent omens increased the sense of panic. An owl was seen in the city, and caught. A statue poured with sweat for three days. A meteor crossed above the city from south to east. Thunderbolts, turfs, stones, flints, and gouts of blood were observed flying through the air. There had still been no elections for the year when both Milo and Clodius were removed from the reckoning. Milo was to be prosecuted for murder; his victim was Clodius.

On 18 January, Clodius was returning on horseback from Aricia along the Appian Way, accompanied by two friends and some slaves. As they passed

*Figure 6.2* Silver *denarius* of 48 BC, showing (obverse) a prisoner representing
Gaul and a Celtic trumpet with an animal's head, the *carnyx*. On the
reverse, Artemis, the Greek name for Diana, goddess of light and also
of the hunt, holds a spear in her left hand, while her right hand is on
the head of a stag; the name Hostilius Saserna is that of the moneyer.
(× 2)

Milo, with his wife and entourage, going in the opposite direction, there was
an altercation followed by a brawl. Clodius was wounded in the shoulder and
taken to a nearby inn. Milo, reckoning that Clodius would now be an even more
dangerous enemy to have around, had him thrown out of the inn and killed.

A senator who happened to be passing picked up the body and brought it
back to Rome, where Clodius's wife Fulvia and his political cronies incited
the mob to riot. His body was carried by tribunes in state to the forum,
where it was cremated in a fire so fierce that it also incinerated the senate
house. Milo's house was attacked, as was that of Marcus Aemilius Lepidus's
son, the *interrex* in the absence of elected consuls. The senate pronounced a
state of emergency, and Pompey, the man on the spot, was appointed sole
consul. Proceedings were brought against Milo. He was defended by Cicero
who, however, was so unnerved by the dead man's vociferous claque and by
the fact that Pompey had ringed the place with armed soldiers, that he did
not make the speech which he had prepared. Milo was duly convicted and
sentenced to exile, which he chose to spend in Marseilles. Cicero sent him a
copy of the speech he never delivered; Milo replied that he was glad that
Cicero had not actually done so, otherwise he would never have had the
opportunity of enjoying the red mullet which was such a speciality of
Marseilles.

From being emergency leader of the state, Pompey transformed himself
effortlessly into constitutional consul. First, however, it was arranged that all
ten tribunes would bring in a bill (known as the law of the ten tribunes) by
which Caesar was enabled to stand for the consulship *in absentia*, while still in
command in Gaul, and thus avoid possible prosecution in between offices for
past acts. Then Pompey, having taken as consular colleague his new father-
in-law, Metellus Scipio, embarked on a series of measures designed to shore

up aspects of the ramshackle constitution. A law *de iure magistratuum* stated unequivocally that all candidates for office must appear in person. When it was pointed out to Pompey that this would seem to contradict the law of the ten tribunes, he added a clause to the effect that the provisions did not apply to Caesar, though he was probably aware that the original law would overrule any subsequent provisions until it was formally repealed.

He also sponsored a law which made compulsory a five-year gap between holding an office and taking up a provincial post. This was designed to curb rampant bribery at the polls, the cost of which successful candidates for consul or praetor could shortly afterwards recover from the inhabitants of the province to which they were posted. This law could have caused problems to Caesar. It certainly discomfited Cicero because, with so many former officials now temporarily disqualified from serving in the provinces, he found himself sent as governor to Cilicia. Pompey did not omit to promote his personal interests, however, for he had his own Spanish command extended for a further five years.

The anarchy in Rome which followed the murder of Clodius reverberated throughout Gaul, generating a new resolve on the part of the insurgents, and a new threat. A plan was forged to cause the maximum amount of embarrassment to Rome and to strike fear into all Roman civilians working in Gaul. At sunrise one day, with Caesar in his province the other side of the Alps, the Carnutes struck at the heart of his lines of supply by massacring the Roman merchants at their commercial base of Orleans, a significant centre of the corn trade. At the same time, the confederacy of tribes hostile to Rome had now found a charismatic leader in Vercingetorix of the Arverni, whose father, according to Caesar himself, had been chief over all Gaul.

If the Celts imagined that they could somehow prevent Caesar from rejoining his legions, who were wintering in the north-east of Gaul, they reckoned without him. A senatorial decree calling for the enlistment of all Italian young men of military age gave him carte blanche to raise another legion in Cisalpine Gaul, with which, and whatever bodyguard he had with him, he crossed the Alps into Transalpine Gaul. Here he set in train the raising of a further legion whose original function was to protect the northern border of the province in the present state of emergency – it was subsequently known as the Fifth *Alaudae* (Larks).

Meanwhile Vercingetorix, with the moral backing of most of the tribes of Gaul, was forging a cohesive army. Having taken hostages from them, he requisitioned fighting men, especially cavalry, and arms. He instilled discipline into his troops by a system of harsh punishment for disobedience. For a major transgression, the perpetrator was first tortured and then burned to death; minor offenders had their ears cut off or one eye gouged out and then were sent home as an example to others. He was personally putting pressure on the Bituriges to join his cause while Caesar was considering his own options. If he ordered any of his regular legions to join him, there was a risk

*Figure 6.3* Silver *denarius* of 48 BC showing (obverse) a head which might represent Vercingetorix and a Celtic shield. On the reverse is a two-horse Celtic chariot with driver and warrior, of a kind which caused Caesar problems in Britain. The moneyer is L. Hostilius Saserna. (× 2)

that they would have to fight a battle on the way without him. If he set out to meet them, he was jeopardizing his personal safety.

Being Caesar, he marched, with his untrained levy, and suddenly irrupted into Arvernian territory across the Cevennes, through passes which at that time of year were two metres deep in snow. It was a feint. While Vercingetorix hastily made his way back to his home ground, Caesar led his rudimentary force northwards to the Seine, where he had ordered his regular legions to concentrate. Then, with his full complement, he recrossed the Loire to attack Avaricum, the heavily-fortified settlement of the Bituriges.

Outwitted in the initial exchanges, Vercingetorix changed his strategy to one of attrition. The Romans were to be denied access to food supplies. While the Bituriges insisted that Avaricum should be spared, 20 other of their significant settlements were deliberately set on fire in a scorched earth policy which also included villages and farmsteads. Caesar was forced to send foraging parties on widely scattered missions, while Vercingetorix and his men hovered around, picking them off. Then, while Caesar considered how to take Avaricum, Vercingetorix camped some 16 miles away.

With no chance of starving the inhabitants out before his troops ran out of food, Caesar resorted to siege engines, and constructed a ramp up to the top of the town wall. The people within retaliated by hurling balls of lighted pitch to set the apparatus on fire, and by tunnelling underneath it to cause more havoc. Caesar brought up his mechanical dart-throwers, but whenever a Gaul on the wall was shot, another took his place. Even with food supplies getting dangerously low, his legionaries insisted on continuing the work:

They had served many years under [Caesar's] command without disgracing themselves or ever leaving any assignment unfinished: it would be shameful to give up this siege once they had begun it. Better to suffer any indignity than fail to avenge the Roman citizens who had lost their lives at Orleans at the hands of the treacherous

Gauls. They asked Caesar to convey the same message on their behalf
to the centurions and tribunes of the army.

*The Gallic War* VII. 17

An attempt by the armed forces in the town, instigated by Vercingetorix,
to escape by night was foiled by their womenfolk, who, failing to persuade
the men not to leave, ruined their plans by shouting them down to the
Romans below. The final assault took place in heavy rain. Of the 40,000
inhabitants of the town, fewer than 800 escaped the inevitable slaughter;
these had leaped from the walls when the first shouts went up. Vercingetorix
rallied his shaken supporters by explaining that it had not been his idea to
fortify the town, and that if the Bituriges had suffered from their insistence
on doing so, it was their own fault. He would, however, continue to strive to
unite the whole of Gaul under one banner.

Among those whose support for Rome was already wavering were the
Aedui, both political wings of whom finally defected after Caesar's next
major engagement, at Gergovia in the territory of the Arverni. He had divided his army in two, sending Labienus north with four legions to put down
a revolt by the Parisii and Senones. Since the situation of Gergovia was such
that he could neither assault it nor besiege it, he finally decided on a tactical
ruse designed to demoralize if not also destabilize the opposition. His main
camp was to the south-east of the town, which was on a plateau. To the south
of the town, facing the Gallic encampments in front of which the Gauls had
built a two-metre dry-stone wall, he constructed a second, smaller, camp,
linked to the main camp by a double trench, each element of which was four
metres wide, so that troops could pass between the two camps without being
observed. The stratagem was to draw Vercingetorix's Gallic troops out to the
west of Gergovia by a diversion. The main body of Caesar's troops, infiltrated
along the communication trenches, would attack and destroy the Gallic
camps from the south and then retire, while the dubiously loyal Aedui would
contribute to the confusion by advancing against the town from the east.
Caesar himself would be in reserve with the Tenth Legion, in a position to
respond to whatever the situation demanded.

The diversion itself was a masterpiece of improvisation. During the night
Caesar dispatched several troops of cavalry towards the hill to the west of the
town, with instructions to make themselves as conspicuous as possible. At
daybreak he ordered his mule drivers to remove the packs from their animals,
put on helmets, and ride, with a few genuine cavalry interspersed between
them, by a more roundabout route in the same direction. To add to the
deception, he moved one of his legions over to his left, where, having been
seen by the opposition on the heights, it was to conceal itself in the woods.

Initially the plan worked to perfection. Vercingetorix took his troops out
of their camps to meet a supposed attack from the west up the slope of the
Heights of Risolles. Caesar's main body of troops rushed the Gallic camps

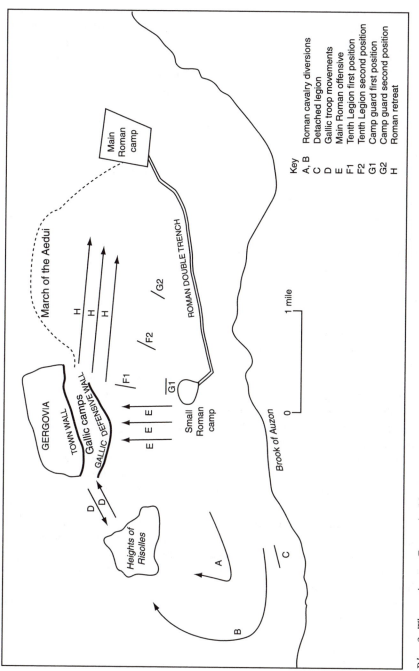

Key

A, B    Roman cavalry diversions
C       Detached legion
D       Gallic troop movements
E       Main Roman offensive
F1      Tenth Legion first position
F2      Tenth Legion second position
G1      Camp guard first position
G2      Camp guard second position
H       Roman retreat

GERGOVIA

TOWN WALL

Gallic camps

GALLIC DEFENSIVE WALL

Main Roman camp

March of the Aedui

ROMAN DOUBLE TRENCH

Small Roman camp

Heights of Risolles

Brook of Auzon

0        1 mile

*Plan 2*: The action at Gergovia 52 BC

with such speed that Teutomatus, king of the Nitiobriges, was literally caught napping in his tent while taking his siesta, and had to escape in a state of undress. With the mission accomplished, Caesar ordered his trumpeters to sound the withdrawal. His soldiers, either because their blood was up or because they genuinely did not hear the call, pressed on to the walls of the town; some even managed to get themselves inside. There was panic within. Women on the battlements showered the troops below with clothing and silver coins, showed their breasts, and stretched out their hands, imploring the Romans not to treat them as they had the women and children of Avaricum. Some even had themselves lowered from the wall and offered themselves to the soldiers.

As soon as Vercingetorix realized what was happening, he sent his troops streaming in against the now disorganized Roman left. The chaos in the ranks was increased by the appearance over to the Roman right of the massed lines of the Aedui, who were mistaken by some to be Vercingetorix's Gallic reinforcements. Caesar was forced to use the Tenth and the cohorts guarding the smaller camp to cover the enforced retreat, in the course of which he lost 46 centurions and 700 legionaries.

The Romans, who had been hoping for a favourable drawn result, had to settle instead for a technical defeat. The next day Caesar assembled his troops and lectured them on military tactics and the importance of obeying orders. Then he led his legions out of camp and on to favourable ground, where he drew them up in line of battle. Vercingetorix refused to be drawn. The two sides went their own ways, Vercingetorix to instil new fire into his troops and to establish his authority over the Aedui, who had now come over to him, Caesar to meet up with Labienus, who had to battle his way across the Seine to make the rendezvous to the north of the Loire.

Vercingetorix now made his base the almost impregnable fortress city of Alesia, peopled by the Mandubii, and deputed the Aedui to make sorties against Caesar's province of Transalpine Gaul. Caesar appointed his second cousin, Lucius Julius Caesar, to defend the province by spreading out along its frontiers cohorts from the new legion which had been raised locally. Then, having rested his legions and found sufficient sources of food, he set out with them to take charge of the operation himself. In order to redress the imbalance between the regular cavalry commanded by Vercingetorix and the auxiliary horsemen at his disposal, Caesar had ordered reinforcements from the Germanic tribes across the Rhine whom he had recently subdued. When they arrived, he decided that their horses were too light for the job, and remounted their riders on horses commandeered from his military tribunes, veterans who had volunteered to re-enlist and thus qualified to ride on the march, and other mounted personnel.

Vercingetorix decided temporarily to abandon his guerrilla tactics in favour of an all-out assault on Caesar's line of march while it was encumbered with the baggage train. Astonishingly, Caesar seems to have been caught by surprise as three contingents of Gallic cavalry swept out of nowhere and engaged his column on the flanks and at its head. He ordered his cavalry out in three divisions to combat the triple threat, while the legions formed up in hollow squares protecting the baggage. Where he saw any of his lines begin to buckle, Caesar signalled for the standards to be brought forward and the troops to advance in battle formation. The conflict was at its height when Caesar's newly acquired and rehorsed German cavalry, having made their way round to the top of a nearby ridge, suddenly thundered down and threw the Gallic horse back against their own infantry, waiting in reserve with Vercingetorix to apply the *coup de grâce*.

So far in the campaign, Vercingetorix had got most things right, against an inspirational strategist. Also, of all the tribes in Gaul, only three still supported Caesar. At this point, however, perhaps unsettled at the indignity of losing an engagement he had promised to win, Vercingetorix made his first and, as it turned out, his last tactical error. He withdrew, with his cavalry and about 80,000 infantry, to Alesia, which stood on a plateau bounded on three sides by rivers. Caesar took up the challenge, and established a blockade of the city, which he surrounded with an elaborate series of ditches and earthworks (contravallation). To protect his troops from attacks by a relieving force, he then constructed a further ring of fortifications outside the first (circumvallation).

Vercingetorix made several sorties out of the gates, but his men were severely mauled by Caesar's German cavalry. To save food, and also to summon assistance, he managed to get his cavalry out by night, with instructions to raise the tribes. Both sides were now running short of supplies. One of Vercingetorix's lieutenants advocated killing the elderly people of the city and eating them. A compromise was reached. All civilians, Mandubii who had given hospitality to Vercingetorix and his forces, with their wives and children, were turned out of the gates. Caesar posted armed sentries on the ramparts and refused to let them through the Roman lines, leaving them to starve in no-man's land.

The Gallic relieving force duly arrived and encamped on the heights to the west of the city. To preserve unity and discipline, the chiefs had decided against a general levy, but instead to enlist a quota of troops from each tribe, according to its population. Among those elected to lead the joint force was Commius, king of the Gallic Atrebates, his past loyalty to Rome now forgotten in an access of bitter hatred. In all, according to figures supplied to or by Caesar, it numbered 250,000 infantry and 8000 cavalry, against Caesar's 10 legions and attendant cavalry, who also had to contend, of course, with the Gallic forces inside Alesia.

There were two battles, one by day and the other by night. Caesar, conspicuous in the red cloak of commander-in-chief, was forced to fight both on two fronts. While the relieving forces assailed the Roman outer line of defences at various points, Vercingetorix with his warriors made sallies out of

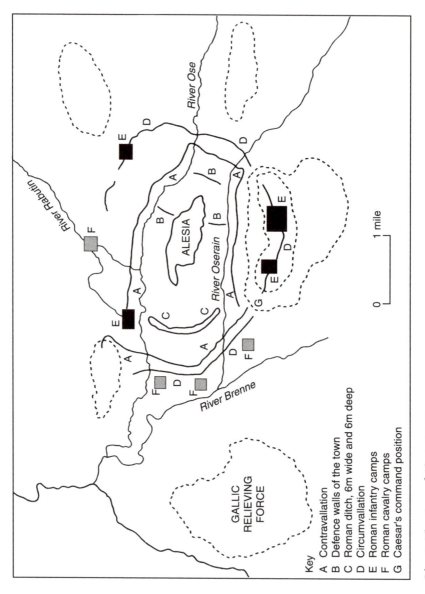

Key
A  Contravallation
B  Defence walls of the town
C  Roman ditch, 6m wide and 6m deep
D  Circumvallation
E  Roman infantry camps
F  Roman cavalry camps
G  Caesar's command position

0                    1 mile

*Plan 3*: The siege of Alesia 52 BC

the city against the inner line. Caesar himself led the final *coup de main*, appearing with four cohorts and a troop of cavalry to reinforce an attack on the Gallic rear. There was wholesale slaughter, and surrender. Vercingetorix was handed over, and sent to Rome in chains. Commius escaped. Caesar spared members of the Aedui and Arverni, to make it easier to recover their territories for the empire. The rest of the prisoners he distributed as booty to his troops, one per man.

Alesia marked the end of concerted Gallic resistance, but not quite the end of hostilities. Pockets of resistance still had to be mopped up or prevented from materializing. For this reason, Caesar wintered in Bibracte. On the last day of 52 BC, he rode out of the camp with an escort of cavalry, leaving his 31-year-old quartermaster-general, Mark Antony, in charge. Collecting two legions from their winter quarters on his way, he invaded the territory of the Bituriges, whom he harassed mercilessly for a month, and then treated magnanimously, in order to demonstrate that it was better to be a friend than an enemy of Rome. He was equally merciful to the Bellovaci, who were planning, in conjunction with Commius's Atrebates, to overcome the Suessiones, a dependent tribe of the Remi, who had remained loyal to Caesar. This campaign was short, and tricky, and once again Commius himself got away.

It was possibly because there was at large a potential focus of a new uprising, that the name of Ambiorix of the Eburones began to be heard again. Whether or not he was still alive, Caesar reacted instantly: 'He sent legions or auxiliary detachments into all parts of the territory ruled by Ambiorix, which he destroyed by wholesale slaughter, fire, and plunder' (*The Gallic War* VIII. 25).

Commius, having persistently been hunted down, and having narrowly avoided being murdered by a Roman peace mission, was finally wounded in a skirmish and surrendered to Mark Antony. He was allowed to go free, however, after vowing never again to look a Roman in the face. Sextus Julius Frontinus (*c.* AD 40–103), governor of Britain and technical writer, has a subsequent anecdote in his book about military tactics:

> Commius, of the Atrebates, having been defeated by the divine Julius, was escaping from Gaul on his way to Britain, and embarked when the wind happened to be fair, but the tide was out. Though his ships were stranded in the shoals, he nevertheless ordered their sails to be unfurled. Caesar, following from a distance, saw the sails swelling in the brisk breeze and, thinking Commius was happily on his way, gave up the chase.
>
> *Stratagems* II. 13. 11

Whether or not the story is true, or even based on fact, Commius did escape to Britain, where he founded a dynasty of tribal kings south of the river Thames.

Caesar employed the same ruthlessness against a band of rebels who had holed themselves up in Uxellodunum, as he had with the Eburones. When he arrived at the town on a hill-top plateau, the siege was already under way. He summed up the position, and by posting in strategic positions skilled bowmen and slingers from his auxiliary troops and artillery, cut off the town from its principal water supply, a tributary of the river Dordogne in the valley below. There was still, however, a spring close beneath the edge of the plateau. Under a continuous barrage of burning barrels filled with pitch and grease rolled down from above, Caesar's engineers managed to divert the spring at its source by digging underground tunnels. The inhabitants of the town capitulated.

> Caesar knew that his merciful nature was well known, and had no concern that severer treatment on his part might be seen as innate cruelty. At the same time, he could not envisage a successful outcome to his policies if many others in various parts indulged in similar measures. He reckoned that the rest must be deterred by an exercise of exemplary punishment. So, while granting them their lives, he amputated the hands of all who had borne arms, to demonstrate more clearly the penalties for criminal activity.
>
> [Aulus Hirtius] *The Gallic War* VIII, 44

At some point during 51 BC Caesar transferred the Fifteenth Legion to Cisalpine Gaul, on the grounds that it was needed there in case of any trouble from beyond the frontiers of Illyricum. During the winter of 51/50 BC, he remained in Transalpine Gaul, establishing administrative guidelines for the new province of Gaul. The tribes were allowed to continue as individual states. He levied a nominal tribute from second-class tribes who had shown overt opposition to Rome: nominal, because they could not afford more in the impoverished state to which they had been reduced. He had achieved in Gaul a sort of peace, on his own terms, and he had added to the Roman empire a territory twice the size of Italy, with a population far greater than that of Spain. By making the Rhine the eastern frontier of the new province, he made it possible for a French nation to evolve from a predominantly Celtic society overlaid with Latin culture. He enriched the Roman empire while at the same time enriching himself. According to Suetonius, he had been plundering temples large and small of the votive offerings deposited with them, and had been in the habit of looting towns because their inhabitants were rich, rather than because they had opposed him. By these and other means he collected more gold than he could handle, and took to selling it for silver in Italy and in other parts of the empire at about two-thirds of the official rate of exchange. Much of his new wealth went towards fuelling his celebrated generosity, especially to his staff, and to those who might be useful to him, including their slaves and freedmen. He also had the pay of legionaries doubled, to 225 *denarii* a year – there were four sesterces to one *denarius*.

Now, at the age of 49, he could concentrate on his own immediate future. His intention was to stand two years hence as consul for 48 BC, without leaving his provincial command, for which there was some legal precedent. Pompey, the arch-rival of any plans by which Caesar might promote his own interests, was ensconced in Italy: 'Caesar could not stand any longer someone above him, / Nor could Pompey abide anyone being his equal' (Lucan, *The Civil War* I. 125–6). The ranks of Caesar's political opponents were now reinforced by those who had realized that on balance they would prefer no repeat of the autocratic consulship of 59 BC.

Marcus Claudius Marcellus, consul in 51 BC, had opened the campaign for the anti-Caesarians by proposing that as the Gallic campaign was now over, Caesar should be replaced with immediate effect. Though tribunes, probably acting on Caesar's instructions, gave notice that they would veto any such suggestion, the senate agreed to Marcus Marcellus's alternative proposal that the matter should be discussed on 1 March 50 BC. Marcus Marcellus also chose a peculiarly brutal and graphic method of illustrating his contempt for Caesar's prestige. One of the measures of Publius Vatinius which had been formally approved in 59 BC authorized Caesar to found a Roman colony at Novum Comum, north of the Po, whose inhabitants he had treated as Roman citizens. Marcus Marcellus declared the measure invalid and, to prove his point, had a senator of the colony flogged (a punishment never inflicted on Roman citizens) and told to go and show his stripes to Caesar.

Caesar badly needed some practical help at the centre. With his unerring judgment of character, he chose Gaius Scribonius Curio, a bankrupt member of the nobility who was a tribune of the people in 50 BC. In the past Curio had shared drinking, gambling, and sexual escapades with Mark Antony, and had been a close associate of Clodius, whose widow Fulvia was now his wife. In return for the settlement of all his debts, Curio gladly switched his allegiance from the cause of the *optimates* to that of Caesar, whose interests he promoted with the utmost efficiency. As an additional insurance policy, Caesar bought one of the consuls for 50 BC, Lucius Aemilius Paullus, with a bribe so generous that with just part of it Paullus was able to complete the rebuilding of the Basilica Aemilia in the forum.

The other consul for that year, Gaius Claudius Marcellus, though he was Caesar's great-nephew, being married to Octavia, was an incorruptible advocate of the cause of the *optimates*. When the matter of Caesar's command came up for discussion on 1 March, Curio promptly exercised his veto, and went on exercising it. Curio was unable, however, to anticipate a notable piece of tactical legerdemain on the part of Pompey, when the senate, alarmed at news that the Parthians might be massing for an attack on Syria, ordered him and Caesar each to release one of their legions. Pompey's response was to nominate as his contribution the legion (*Legio I*) he had lent Caesar in 53 BC, thus depriving Caesar of two legions. Caesar complied fully, surrendering of his own troops the Fifteenth Legion, one of his least experienced, from Cisalpine Gaul, and replacing it with the Thirteenth, originally raised by him in 57 BC. To each member both of the Fifteenth and of Pompey's legion he gave a parting bonus of 250 *denarii* (more than a year's pay under the new scale) out of his own pocket. As it turned out, no reinforcements were required on the Syrian front, and the legions remained for the time being at a base at Capua. Gaius Marcellus, concerned that they might be returned to Caesar, took it upon himself to announce that they should stay in Italy and be under Pompey's jurisdiction.

During the summer, in Naples, Pompey was so ill, possibly from malaria, that prayers were offered locally for his survival. His recovery was greeted with such national rejoicing that it went to his head. When asked where the troops were to oppose Caesar, should he march against Rome, he replied, according to Plutarch, ' "Wherever in Italy I stamp my foot upon the ground, armies of infantry and cavalry will rise up" ' (*Pompey* 57).

Early in September Caesar put Labienus in command of the Thirteenth Legion in Cisalpine Gaul, and travelled back to Gaul, where he quartered four legions in the territory of the Belgae, and four among the Treveri. He had also the 22 cohorts comprising the Fifth *Alaudae* in the province of Transalpine Gaul.

On 1 December 50 BC, Curio moved in the senate that both Pompey and Caesar should simultaneously give up their commands, which was carried by 370 votes to 22. Whereupon Gaius Marcellus dismissed the meeting in a fury, with the words, ' "You have won your cause, and become Caesar's slaves" ' (Appian, *Civil Wars* II. 30).

The following day, Gaius Marcellus, accompanied by the two consuls-elect for 49 BC, Gaius Claudius Marcellus, brother of Marcus Marcellus, and Cornelius Lentulus, and the discomfited *optimates* who had voted against the motion, went to Pompey's house outside the city limits. There, without being empowered to do so by the senate, they invited Pompey to defend the state, giving him command of the two legions at Capua and the authority to raise more. Pompey accepted.

For every catastrophe such as a war, and especially a civil war, there are several causes. There is no doubt that Curio's motion was intended to play into Caesar's hands, for he had the popular vote, he had his legions, and he was, for his successes in Gaul, the man of the hour. Cicero, back in Italy from Cilicia, where he had notched up an improbable military victory against a group of mountain guerrillas, recognized this:

> I greatly fear for the state. Up till now I have hardly found anyone who does not think that Caesar should be conceded what he wants, rather than go to war. What he asks is, indeed, impudent, but more valid than had been supposed. Why, however, should we now begin

standing out against him? *In truth, is any evil worse today* [Homer, *Odyssey* xii. 209] than when we extended his command for another five years, or when we let him stand for election without being present, unless perhaps we gave him these weapons so as to fight today against someone well prepared?

*To Atticus* VII. 6

Curio, whose powers as a tribune were limited to within the city limits and whose office was due to expire on 10 December, reported to Caesar in Ravenna. Caesar now had with him, in addition to the Thirteenth Legion, the 22 cohorts and some cavalry from Transalpine Gaul; he had also ordered the Eighth and the Twelfth legions to march from their winter quarters in Gaul to join him. Still trying to find a peaceful solution, he sent a message to Pompey offering to surrender his interests and his legions in Gaul, if he could retain his provinces of Cisalpine Gaul and Illyricum with two legions until he entered on his consulship. Pompey was quite happy with this, but the consuls rejected it. Caesar made his final offer in a letter to the senate. It was entrusted to Curio, who covered the 270 miles to Rome in three days, and handed it personally to the new consuls as they were entering the conference hall for the inaugural meeting of the session on 1 January 49 BC.

The letter comprised a dignified statement of what Caesar had achieved from the beginning of his career and a proposal that he was willing to surrender his command at the same time as Pompey, with the rider that if Pompey did not give up that command, he would come down with all speed and avenge the wrongs which had been done to his country and to himself.

Appian, *Civil Wars* II. 32

After the letter had, against interruptions, been read aloud, there was an uproar, during which Cornelius Lentulus refused to debate its terms, and called instead for a discussion on the general political situation. Pompey's father-in-law, Metellus Scipio, now proposed that if Caesar did not surrender his command by a certain date, he would be declared a public enemy. An overwhelming majority voted in favour, but the motion was vetoed by Mark Antony and Quintus Cassius Longinus, recently elected as tribunes for 49 BC.

Cicero, who had been awarded a triumph for his military campaign in the mountains of Cilicia, was thus prevented from entering the city, but he participated in meetings at Pompey's house. While Pompey seemed sympathetic to his proposals for a compromise, Cornelius Lentulus and Cato were adamant that none could be entertained. On 7 January, the senate, having formally but unconstitutionally rejected the tribunes' veto, appointed Ahenobarbus to take over Caesar's command in Transalpine Gaul, with the authority to raise 4000 troops in Italy. That done, a *senatus consultum ultimum* was issued, protecting the state from unlawful actions against it. In this at least, the senate was within its rights.

A veneer of legality had now been applied to the culmination of a long sequence of more or less disgraceful episodes in the history of the republic, all of which centred on power. Unless Caesar meekly gave up his command and as a private citizen laid himself open to prosecution, which would undoubtedly follow, he was in law an enemy of the state. There was no way back for a Roman whose *dignitas* had been affronted to such an extent, especially one whose essential make-up included a certain amount of arrogance justifiable in a public figure of his talents and achievements. The senate must have known this.

With Pompey already waiting on stage if Caesar should miss his cue, the consuls ordered Antony and Quintus Cassius out of the senate for their own safety. With Curio, they escaped from the city in a hired carriage, disguised as slaves. On their arrival at Caesar's camp, he exhibited them to the troops exactly as they were, without allowing them to wash or change. This, he said, is the way the republic treats honourable men who have stood up for your rights.

The civil war which no-one, except perhaps the 22 hardline senators, really wanted had effectively begun. The senate now held the constitutional high ground. The onus was on Caesar, if he wished to prolong the diplomatic process, to demonstrate that the military advantages were with him. The senate immediately granted Pompey all the money in the public treasury plus the private fortunes of its members, if needed, and authorized Pompey to raise an army from Italy of 130,000 men with experience in war. Caesar, however, instead of waiting, as his opponents expected, to concentrate more of his troops in northern Italy, dumbfounded them with one of his tactical hallmarks. He split the Thirteenth Legion into two detachments and ordered lightning strikes against the principal towns of Umbria and Etruria.

First, however, there was a piece of constitutional folklore to be registered indelibly in the annals of history. The river Rubicon, by an administrative accident, was the northern limit of the environs of the town of Ariminum (now Rimini). It was also the boundary between the province of Cisalpine Gaul and Italy. By law, Caesar could not leave his province without losing his command; to bring armed soldiers into Italy was an act of aggression against the state.

The accounts of the ancient historians differ only in detail and in the precise sequence of events. Suffice to say that however Caesar arrived at the north bank of the river just before dawn on 11 January 49 BC, he almost certainly paused at the bridge. According to the sources, what he actually said before crossing it was in the form of a metaphor from the game of dice: 'The die is cast,' reflecting the modern croupier's cry, '*Rien ne va plus*,' or else 'Let the die be cast.' Whichever it was, Caesar chose to illustrate his symbolic gesture by indulging in his penchant for classical quotations: he spoke in Greek, quoting from a lost play of Menander.

CICERO

# THE DICTATOR

## Civil War 49–48 BC

> So, they devised their battle tactics against each other, and then
> did the rounds of their lines, attending to necessary preliminar-
> ies, inciting the troops to show courage, and passing on the
> rallying cry, which in Caesar's case was 'Venus Victorious' and
> in Pompey's 'Hercules the Unbeatable'.
>
> Appian, *Civil Wars* II. 76

Ariminum fell, and then Pisaurum, Fanum, and Ancona, on the main east-
coast road, while Mark Antony occupied Arretium. As Curio advanced on
Iguvium, the garrison holding it defected to Caesar's side. In Rome, there
was consternation; those outside came rushing in, and those inside desper-
ately tried to get out. To assert some semblance of rational command, Pompey
ordered the evacuation of the city and himself beat a strategic retreat to
Capua, where he instructed the consuls and senate to reconvene.

Caesar's own account of his campaigns in 49 and 48 BC is *Bellum Civile*
(The Civil War), a title which he is unlikely to have given it himself. Much
more than *The Gallic War*, it is an attempt to justify his actions in political
terms, and must be treated with some caution as regards its historical

authenticity. The other contemporary source of information is observations made by Cicero in his letters, in the course of which he sometimes betrays an overexcitable nature. It does appear, however, that Pompey had made one final attempt for peace, dispatching to Ariminum two envoys, Lucius Caesar, the son of Caesar's deputy in Transalpine Gaul, and Lucius Roscius Fabatus, a praetor, with a personal letter to Caesar. Pompey apologized if he had caused any personal affront while acting in the interests of the state, and begged Caesar, in the interests of the state, to return to his province. Caesar apparently replied that he would do so if Pompey would take himself off to Spain, and if both their armies were disbanded, all troops in Italy disarmed, and free elections held under the auspices of the senate and the people of Rome. He further proposed a summit meeting between himself and Pompey to resolve any difficulties.

The envoys reported back to Capua, where Pompey, the consuls, and those senators who had made the rendezvous responded by announcing that if Caesar would first disarm his forces and return to Gaul, Pompey would then go to Spain. In the meantime, the state would carry on enlisting troops in Italy to combat the attack on the constitution mounted by Caesar. Neither side, with some justification, trusted the other. So the deadlock persisted, and the civil war continued on its preordained course.

At the start the two sides were on land numerically about even. Pompey had ten legions, seven in Spain, under two doughty commanders, and three in Italy, of which one consisted of newly enlisted troops, and the other two had until recently been under Caesar's command. Caesar complained bitterly that these two had been filched from him, and Pompey had warned the senate that he doubted their loyalty if they were required to fight against Caesar; small wonder, in the light of the fact that Caesar had bribed them with bounties. Pompey could also call on detachments of troops stationed in outlying parts of the empire such as Africa, Asia, and Syria. Caesar had nine legions, of which the Fifth and Thirteenth were already in Italy, and the Eighth and Twelfth were on the march to join him.

In strategic terms, Caesar was vulnerable on his western front from an attack by Pompey's legions in Spain. This meant that Pompey could draw him to engage in hostilities in the east while having to protect his forces from counter-attacks from behind. Caesar's war fleet, if it was still in active commission, was concentrated off the coast of northern Gaul. Pompey had access, according to Plutarch, to 500 warships and numerous light galleys and reconnaissance vessels, many of them positioned in strategic ports around the Mediterranean. Pompey also achieved a tactical and public relations coup when Titus Labienus defected to him. Labienus had been Pompey's man before he had been Caesar's, and his political background may have swayed him to support the constitution. Caesar's response was typical; he derisively forwarded to Labienus his kit and the cash he had acquired during the campaign.

In other respects, however, the antagonists were unevenly matched, and the war, though fought on several fronts, was a one-sided affair. Pompey was now 56, at a time when many males, if they survived childhood, died in their twenties or thirties. He had seen no active service since 62 BC, and he had been seriously ill the previous summer. He had the power to raise legions in Italy, but it is one thing to enlist troops, another to train them to fight against Roman regulars. Almost all Caesar's legions were battle hardened and in full training after a war which they had decisively won. They were fiercely loyal to their commander, who as a general had proved that he was not only a master tactician and a great leader, but that he was favoured by fortune. To the troops and their centurions, this was an irresistible combination of qualities.

Caesar was 50, but he was supremely fit – the mild form of epilepsy does not yet seem to have afflicted him. He was used to making instant decisions. His surprise tactics had given him a strategic advantage which he had no intention of relinquishing. It was a different kind of war altogether from any that he had engaged in before. He was not opposed to the government; indeed, he needed whatever backing he could constitutionally obtain and he depended on its support for his future. The fight was between two men and their forces, and, in a conflict between two parties whose allegiance owed more to personalities than to principles, he recognized that it was more advantageous to bring the opposition over to his side than to destroy it.

His advance was inexorable, and on 17 February, having been joined now by the Eighth and Twelfth legions and several of Pompey's cohorts which had deserted to him, he was encamped at the crucial crossroads town of Corfinium, some 70 miles from Rome by road. It was held for the government by Lucius Domitius Ahenobarbus with about 30 cohorts. Significantly, among its inhabitants were 50 senators, military tribunes, and equestrians, including Publius Lentulus Spinther, consul in 57 BC. Four days later, before it was light, Spinther shouted down from the wall that he wished to have an interview with Caesar. When he was brought before the *imperator*, he began at once to plead for his life in the course of a long dissertation on their former friendship and the benefits he had earned through Caesar in the past.

Caesar cut him short, pointing out that 'he had not left his province out of any sinister motives, but to defend himself against the insults of his personal enemies, restore to their lawful positions the tribunes of the people who had recently been expelled while exercising their constitutional rights, and free himself and the people of Rome from the tyranny of a minority' (*The Civil War* I. 22). He then sent Spinther back into the town to reassure the others who had feared for their personal safety. At dawn, Corfinium capitulated. Caesar had the 50 prominent citizens of Rome lined up before him, and ordered his troops who were standing by to cease jeering. Then he let them go free. He also returned to Ahenobarbus the six million sesterces of public money which the town magistrates had handed over to him, though he knew it had been allocated by Pompey to pay the troops. The men themselves he enlisted under oath in his own army, before moving on.

Caesar's military strategy he was keeping to himself. His political policy he now outlined in a letter to Balbus and Oppius:

> Let us try by exercising moderation to regain the good will of all and achieve a lasting victory, since others, by employing cruelty, have been unable to avoid being hated or to retain for very long the upper hand, except of course for Sulla, whom I do not propose to emulate. This is a new victory rationale, to fortify our position with kindly and generous intentions.
>
> Quoted in Cicero, *To Atticus* IX. 7c

This was written 'on the march'. Pompey had withdrawn to Brundisium, with his two legions and whatever other troops he could find, with the intention of embarking with them for Greece, and there to regroup his forces. Caesar followed him, sending ahead messages asking for talks. Pompey ignored them. On the way Caesar captured one of Pompey's commanders and two of his chief engineers, all of whom he promptly released.

By the time Caesar arrived at Brundisium, Pompey had got half his army away, while the other half waited for the transports to return. Caesar besieged the town, but was unable to prevent the second embarkation. With Pompey and his army went the consuls and their paraphernalia. Caesar now

*Figure 7.1* Head of Pompey with stylized hair recalling Alexander the Great, from Ny Carlsberg Glyptotek, Copenhagen. (G. Garvey/Ancient Art & Architecture Collection)

headed for Rome, which he had not seen for nine years, leaving his exhausted troops temporarily to recuperate in Apulia. On the way, he stopped off at Formiae, where Cicero had one of his country residences. There was nothing more now for Cicero to do as a mediator. Caesar, however, needed someone of Cicero's stature to back his quasi-constitutional demands, and for this he needed him in Rome, where Cicero had flatly refused to show his face. For Cicero's problem was that the consul who had taken such decisive action in 63 BC simply could not make up his mind whom he should back. He was, however, sufficiently aware of the consequences of the war; whoever won, the constitution would have suffered permanent damage.

Caesar's determination to get Cicero's backing is illustrated by the flurry of correspondence between them over the previous weeks, into which Balbus and Oppius were drawn as Caesar's agents. Though nothing more was ever said, or heard, about Cicero's triumph, in these letters Cicero is studiously addressed as 'Cicero *imperator*', though one wonders whether 'From Caesar *imperator*, greetings to Cicero *imperator*' is intended as flattery or irony. Cicero would undoubtedly have taken it as the former: Caesar was perfectly capable of employing the latter.

Caesar brought matters between them to a head by calling a meeting of the full senate in Rome on 1 April, which he announced by posting up notices in all the towns round about, including Formiae. The face to face meeting which Cicero had tried to avoid took place at his villa on 28 March. Cicero described their conversation to Atticus.

> I took your advice on both counts. My line was to obtain his respect rather than his thanks, while maintaining my determination not to go to Rome. We made a mistake in thinking it would be easy. I have never encountered anything less so. He said again and again that if I did not come, he would suffer personal damage by my decision, and that others would be more reluctant to appear. I pointed out that my situation was different from theirs.
>
> After a great deal more talk, he said, 'So come and discuss peace.'
>
> 'With my own agenda?' I enquired.
>
> 'Do I need to prescribe one for you?'
>
> 'So,' I said, 'I shall propose that the senate does not give its approval for you to campaign in Spain or take an army to Greece. And,' I added, 'I shall loudly deplore anything that happens to Pompey.'
>
> 'I certainly don't want you to take that line,' he replied.
>
> 'So I thought,' I said. 'But I don't want to come because either I must say it, and a great deal more on which I cannot be silent if I am there, or I must stay away.'
>
> The outcome was that I would think it over, as he himself suggested by way of concluding our discussion. I had no alternative. So,

we parted. I am certain he has no liking for me. But I am pleased with myself, as I have not been to such an extent for ages.

*To Atticus* IX, 18

Cicero did not go to Rome. The meeting of senators, it could hardly be called a meeting of the senate, properly convened at the request of the tribunes Mark Antony and Quintus Cassius, was held outside the city limits in deference to Caesar's quasi-legal office as a provincial governor. In a long discourse, calmly delivered, he aimed to disperse his audience's alarm at the train of events and reassure them of his desire for peace. He rehearsed his personal grievances, and proposed that a peace mission should be sent to the consuls and Pompey. He made a similar speech to an assembly of the people, also held outside the city limits, emphasizing his argument by making available extra corn and promising each citizen a handout of 300 sesterces.

In the event, no-one could be found willing to participate in the peace mission, since Pompey had previously announced that anyone who remained in Rome was to be regarded as a member of Caesar's camp. Discussions in the senate went on for three days, with the tribune Lucius Metellus applying his veto to anything that Caesar proposed. To finance his campaign, it was necessary for Caesar to get his hands on the contents of the reserve state treasury in the temple of Saturn. When this, too, was refused, Caesar took an armed escort into the city, threatened to kill Lucius Metellus, who had taken it upon himself to guard the treasury, and, when the keys could not be found, had the place broken into. His haul, 15,000 bars of gold, 30,000 bars of silver, and 30 million sesterces in cash, was considerable, but his action cost him much of his popularity with the public. Indeed, according to Cicero, such was the strength of feeling that Caesar cancelled a public speech that he had intended to make before leaving Rome.

Caesar, in a thoroughly bad mood, now left for Spain with six legions, having put the praetor, Marcus Aemilius Lepidus, son of the consul for 78 BC, in charge of matters in Rome, and Mark Antony in command of the troops in Italy. His aim was to avoid having a dangerous army at his back when he took the fight to Pompey. For the benefit of his staff, he quipped that 'he was going to meet an army without a leader and would return to face a leader without an army' (Suetonius, *Julius Caesar* 34). To secure the supplies of corn without which Italy could not survive, he sent Curio with four legions to take over the provinces of Sicily and Africa. Curio managed the first part of his assignment without trouble. His military inexperience, however, let him down in Africa, where Juba, king of Numidia, saw an opportunity to make trouble by joining the cause of those opposed to Caesar, who had tweaked his beard during a private altercation some 13 years earlier. Curio lost his life and two of his legions in an ambush. He also lost his head, which was cut off and taken to Juba.

Cicero, Caesar's erstwhile friend and sparring partner, had still dithered about what he should do, even after receiving a letter from Caesar, written on the march, which offered him safety if he would remain neutral. Finally, though he did not trust Pompey any more than he trusted Caesar, he sailed for Greece, where he could be of no practical assistance to anyone.

Caesar had in Spain in support of his legions 5000 auxiliary infantry and 3000 cavalry that had served with him in Gaul, and a similar number of each recruited from the Gallic tribes themselves. By an ingenious form of financial sleight of hand, he reinforced the allegiance of his tribunes and centurions by borrowing sums of money from them (which would have to be earned in loyalty if they wanted repayment), and then distributing the takings to the troops as bonuses. The campaign itself, against well-drilled Roman legions under two capable commanders, was decided in 40 days, virtually without bloodshed, just as Caesar had intended. He outmanoeuvred his opponents near Ilerda by a combination of skilled engineering (bridge building and the construction of a ford), ingenuity (making coracles, such as he had seen in Britain, as transports), and surprise forced marches, at the same time as facing serious supply problems. While Afranius and Petreius were deciding what evasive action to take, there was some fraternization between the two sides. Petreius gave orders that any of Caesar's men found in his camp would be executed. Caesar announced that any supporters of Pompey harboured by his men should be well treated and sent back to their own lines, unless they wished to be incorporated in his army. It was a public relations stroke which cost him nothing, and gained him some valuable recruits. For among those who opted to enlist with him were a number of military tribunes and centurions; he welcomed them officially and allowed them to retain their ranks.

Afranius and Petreius were subsequently finessed into a position in the field where surrender was the only sensible course of action. Caesar insisted that the negotiations should be conducted in public, so that his point of view should be heard by the soldiers of both sides. Afterwards, of members of the opposition forces who did not wish to enlist with him, those who came originally from Spain were immediately sent home; the rest were given supplies and discharged on the Var, the river which marked the eastern boundary of Transalpine Gaul.

Caesar left four legions in Spain under Quintus Cassius, to prevent trouble, and sent the rest ahead of him into Italy. He himself returned via Corduba, where he had called a meeting of all communities in Spain, and Cadiz, from which he took a ship to Tarraco. Having dispensed honours to local dignitaries, he travelled overland to Marseilles, where he arrived in September, in time to receive formally the surrender of the city, which had tried to adopt a neutral attitude but had then bowed to the prevailing tide of support for Pompey. The siege had been conducted by Caesar's legate Gaius Trebonius, who had been tribune of the people in 55 BC, and, from the sea, by Decimus Brutus.

While in Marseilles, Caesar learned that Lepidus, on a motion of the people's assembly, had nominated him as dictator, for which it appears there was a constitutional precedent. He had, however, to leave in a hurry for Placentia, where other business called: the Ninth Legion had mutinied. Its members wanted the victory bonus he had promised them before Brundisium, where he had had reason to believe he might end the war in one stroke. They were also unhappy that his lenient attitude towards their opponents was costing them sources of booty. He announced that he had no alternative but to carry out the prescribed punishment of decimation. Since this would involve the execution of about 500 valuable men whom he could ill afford to lose, he allowed himself to be persuaded to show mercy. Instead he had the 120 ringleaders picked out, 12 of whom he condemned to death. One of them proved that he had an alibi for when the mutiny began. Caesar pardoned him and executed in his place the centurion who had made the accusation.

Meanwhile Pompey had been mobilizing and training his forces for an assault on Italy in the spring of 48 BC. His fleet of 600 warships and numerous transports, under the command of Marcus Bibulus, was anchored along the west coast of Greece. He had made up nine legions of Roman citizens from the manpower available to him, while his father-in-law Metellus Scipio, governor of Syria, was on his way from the east with two more. In addition to his legions' attendant auxiliary detachments, Pompey had an extra 3000 archers, 1200 slingers, and 7000 cavalry provided by some of the eastern states. He also had ample supplies of corn, which he had brought in from lands of the east bordering on the Mediterranean.

Caesar sent his 12 legions ahead of him to Brundisium, and travelled to Rome. On his arrival he formally accepted the office of dictator and embarked on a strenuous round of political activity. As presiding officer, he held elections for 48 BC. He himself stood for the consulship and duly announced himself elected with, as his consular colleague, Publius Servilius Isauricus, under whose father he had briefly served in the east in 78 BC. As dictator, he was able to dispense with the senatorial red tape which inevitably attended any attempt to resolve the state's chronic financial situation, and brought in immediate legislation that benefited both debtors and creditors. He organized a distribution of corn to the needy, agreed to the return of all exiles except Milo, and restored the right to stand for office to the sons of those who had been proscribed by Sulla. He also set up the machinery for Roman citizenship at last formally to be granted to the inhabitants of his former province of Cisalpine Gaul.

Having achieved his original aim of the consulship for 48 BC, Caesar was now less amenable to measures for peace. When his father-in-law, Calpurnius Piso, who had been censor in 50 BC, tried to resuscitate in the senate the motion to send a mission to Pompey, Caesar had his colleague as consul-elect, Servilius Isauricus, vote it down. Eleven days after his arrival, he abdicated as dictator, and set off to join his army at Brundisium, having relieved the various temple treasuries of their residual votive offerings. All the way to the city gates he was besieged by people begging him to come to some peaceful arrangement with Pompey. He ignored them. If there was to be any talk of peace, it would be on his terms, not those of the senate or people.

It was almost the end of the year, a close season for maritime operations when no sane Roman would entrust himself to the vagaries of the sea. Caesar's men were exhausted by marching and campaigning. So he stole a march on Pompey by ordering an immediate crossing. There were not enough ships to carry the whole of his army, even close-packed and lightly equipped. He ordered seven legions, including those which had just marched from Spain, to leave their slaves and personal baggage behind, and embark with him. He landed them on the coast of Epirus before Bibulus, lying off Corfu with 100 ships, woke up to what was happening. Bibulus managed to catch 30 of Caesar's transports on their way back to Brundisium, and was in such a rage at his own incompetence that he set fire to them and burned their crews alive.

Mark Antony, in Italy with the rest of the army, including 800 cavalry, and the stragglers who had arrived late, now had to contend not only with the weather but also with the close attentions of Pompey's fleet. For Bibulus was now assiduous in carrying out his command, keeping his fleet at sea and refusing to land from his flagship even when he was so seriously ill from the elements and from exhaustion that he died from lack of medical treatment. At one point Caesar was so frustrated by the delay that he determined to fetch the rest of his troops himself. Disguised in a full cloak, he infiltrated himself into a small boat and ordered its skipper, in Caesar's name, to set sail. As soon as they were out in the open sea a gale blew up and the skipper instructed the helmsman to turn about. Whereupon Caesar revealed himself. ' "Come on, now," ' he shouted, as though this would solve their problems, ' "You're carrying Caesar and all his hopes!" ' (Plutarch, *Julius Caesar* 38). The wind and the storm took no notice and, in spite of the efforts of the oarsmen, the boat was forced to return to shore.

Caesar had managed without trouble to occupy the main towns of Epirus, including Apollonia, thus denying Pompey a base there. Both armies now marched for Dyrrachium, with Pompey's fresher troops winning the race. Caesar withdrew, and camped on the south bank of the river Apsus. Pompey, having reinforced Dyrrachium as a base where he could have supplies brought in by sea, settled his army on the opposite bank, and awaited developments. Caesar, who was forced to send his foraging expeditions ever farther away, would thus be bound to make the first move. The martial intentions of both commanders were almost undone by their troops, who began cheerfully to fraternize across the narrow stretch of water. Caesar, according to his own account, made capital out of the situation by sending his experienced legate Publius Vatinius to make peaceful overtures from his side of the river. These were dashed by Labienus, whose appearance on the opposite bank was the

signal for a shower of missiles from both sides. ' "Stop your talk of a settlement of differences," he shouted. "There can be no peace for us until Caesar's
head has been brought in" ' (*The Civil War* III. 19).

Mark Antony, with four legions and the rest of the cavalry, eventually
sailed in April, but instead of meeting up with Caesar at Apollonia was
forced by a strong south wind to land to the north of Dyrrachium. From that
point, the campaign developed into a game of cat and mouse, with Pompey
gaining further advantage through two outstanding naval feats by Gnaeus
Pompeius Magnus, his elder son, who, in sorties 100 miles apart, at Lissus
and, to the south, Oricum, destroyed the whole of Caesar's fleet.

The two armies eventually faced up to each other along the coast south of
Dyrrachium. There evolved a frantic search on both sides for adequate supplies of food and water, in Pompey's case also for his substantial ranks of
cavalry horse. It was a tactical situation from which Caesar finally extricated
himself only with difficulty after the initial proceedings had lasted for over
two months.

By executing a feint, Caesar established his camp between Pompey and
Dyrrachium, so that Pompey's forces could only be supplied by sea. Caesar,
who had a serious disadvantage in numbers, then built forts on the ring of
surrounding hills, which he linked with earthworks and trenches, restricting
Pompey to the area between them and the sea. In order to give himself as

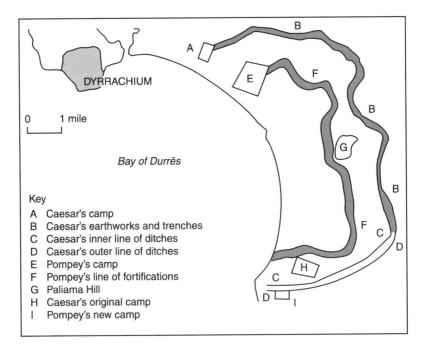

*Plan 4*: Dyrrachium 48 BC

much ground as possible on which to graze his horses, and also to force Caesar repeatedly to lengthen his line and stretch his manpower, Pompey responded with an inner wall of fortifications, ultimately 15 miles long, reinforced with 24 defensive positions. All the time Caesar's men were assailed by Pompey's archers and slingers, from which they were forced to protect themselves with coats of felt, quilt, or hide. When it looked as though Caesar was preparing to drive his line west from Paliama Hill, Pompey took the offensive and forced Mark Antony, who was holding the hill with the Ninth Legion, to give way, and Caesar to extend his fortifications farther to the south.

At one point Caesar's army was so short of supplies that his troops were reduced to making bread from roots. When the opposition, which was well provided with food by ship, taunted them from their side of the fortifications, Caesar's men tossed some of the loaves across to them, to demonstrate their fortitude and determination. Pompey's response, when samples were brought to him, was to exclaim, ' "What brute beasts we are fighting!" ' (Appian, *Civil Wars* II. 61). Caesar was able, however, seriously to disrupt Pompey's water supplies by damming and diverting the springs from the hills.

As the corn began to ripen, Caesar's position improved, while conditions in the restrictions of Pompey's camp became worse, for both men and beasts. Most of the baggage animals had died, and to preserve his cavalry horses Pompey was forced to ship them to Dyrrachium. More than ever confident of the outcome, Caesar made at least three elaborate attempts to detach significant supporters of Pompey from their allegiance. Metellus Scipio was reported to be nearing Macedonia on his march from Syria. Caesar sent to him Aulus Clodius, who had originally joined Caesar's staff on Scipio's recommendation, with a letter to the effect that it lay in Scipio's hands to take the credit for establishing peace and saving the empire. Though there was initially a favourable reaction to this approach, Aulus Clodius was sent back without achieving anything. Cornelius Balbus, nephew of Caesar's agent, took on the hazardous assignment of having talks actually in Pompey's camp with Cornelius Lentulus, consul in 49 BC and subsequently governor of Asia, from which he had brought two legions to Dyrrachium. Lentulus listened, but decided that there was not enough in it for him. Finally, Caesar instructed his lieutenant Publius Cornelius Dolabella, who against Cicero's wishes had married his daughter Tullia, to write to his father-in-law in Pompey's camp, advising him not to follow Pompey to inevitable disaster and reminding him of Caesar's habitual generosity.

Caesar was now inveigled by a double-agent into leaving his camp at night with a light force, believing that the gates of Dyrrachium were going to be opened to him. It was a trap. While Caesar was being attacked in the front and the rear by considerable forces which had been transported there by boat, Pompey launched a triple assault on his camp and lines of fortification.

The position was saved after, according to Caesar, six battles had taken place on a single day. Pompey had used his Cretan archers to devastating effect. Thirty thousand arrows were discharged at one of the defensive positions, in which every man had a wound of some kind and four centurions from one cohort lost their eyes. The shield of another centurion had 120 arrow holes in it, and its owner was still alive. Caesar presented him with a generous bonus and promoted him to *primus pilus*, while all the wounded received double pay, grain, extra rations, and other rewards in kind.

The climax to this aspect of the campaign came after Caesar built two strategic forts near Dyrrachium from which he was able to prevent Pompey's cavalry horses getting out to feed. Pompey was now forced to bring them back again to his camp within his lines of fortification, where forage was scarce. At the southern end of his contravallation, Caesar had constructed a double line of ditches about 200 metres apart. One, which faced Pompey to the north, was about 5 metres wide, and was supported by an earth wall 3 metres high and 3 across, with a palisade. The other, similar but of lesser dimensions, faced south, to discourage any attack from that direction. The lines continued almost to the sea, but had not yet been linked at that end crosswise by any defensive structure. This information was leaked to Pompey by a couple of rogues from Caesar's Gallic cavalry, who had deserted after being charged with embezzling the pay of their own troopers.

The assault from the sea, into the gap between the ditches and against the weaker line from the south, was successful. Simultaneously, 60 of Pompey's cohorts advanced from the north to occupy Caesar's original camp, and Pompey himself, with five legions, landed to the south of Caesar's double line of fortifications and established there a new, permanent camp. Caesar, according to his own account, appeared with 33 cohorts and managed to save the day, at a cost of 32 military tribunes and centurions, 960 men, and 32 standards. In truth, it was a damaging defeat in which many of the dead had been trampled by their comrades as they fled in panic. Pompey was hailed by his troops as *imperator*. Labienus, having taken charge of the prisoners-of-war, had them publicly exhibited and then killed. Caesar disengaged his demoral-ized army, billeted his numerous wounded in Apollonia, and led his fit men into the plains of Thessaly, where the rich cornfields would for the present provide supplies of food. He sent two legions, the Eleventh and Twelfth, and 500 cavalry into Macedonia under Domitius Calvinus, to shadow Metellus Scipio, who was now nearing the end of his long march.

Pompey's basic dilemma was whether to embark his troops for Italy, leav-ing Caesar, who had no ships, the uphill task of returning with his men on foot to attack an army which would be already firmly entrenched there, or whether to go after him and, as it were, kill two birds with one stone. The *optimates* in his entourage persuaded him to do battle, and he marched to join up with his father-in-law before Scipio should be annihilated by the full force of Caesar's legions.

Caesar, in the meantime, having met up with Calvinus, was approaching the town of Gomphi. Pompey had informed the Thessalians that he had scored a decisive victory at Dyrrachium, and so the citizens barred their gates and sent him messengers asking for help. Caesar made an example of the town. He ordered up ladders and, that same day, the high walls of Gomphi were scaled and the town plundered. Appian says that the soldiers, who had suffered much from hunger, ate vastly and drank far too much wine, the German auxiliaries becoming particularly legless. He also describes how the bodies of 20 prominent citizens were found dead on the floor of an apothecary's shop, having taken poison. There was no more trouble from other towns in the region.

The two sides met near Pharsalus. Pompey had a considerable advantage in numbers. His tactics were to maintain pressure on Caesar's infantry all along the line, and then outflank Caesar's right with a massed cavalry attack. Caesar guessed that he would do this, and he guessed right. He removed one cohort from each of his legions' third line, and redeployed them in reserve behind his right wing, hidden from the enemy. At the critical moment these men took up the offensive, using their javelins against the cavalry as bayonets. Pompey's cavalry, caught by surprise at this aggression, interfered with each other, and took flight. Caesar, seeing this, threw his third line, which had not yet engaged the opposition, into the assault. Pompey's infantry

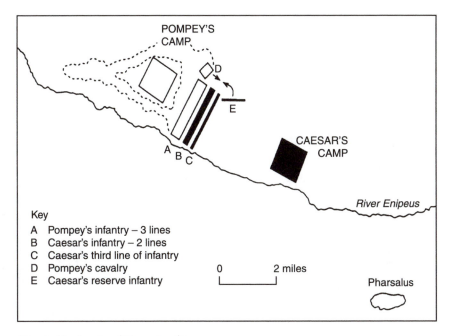

*Plan 5*: The battle of Pharsalus 48 BC

113

could not sustain the fight and fled from the field. At this, Pompey retired to his camp, his nerve so shattered that when Caesar's men broke in, he got on his horse and, with a small escort, galloped into the distance.

Caesar, as he looked on the corpses of the 15,000, including 6000 Roman citizens, who had stayed, and fought, observed, ' "They wished it so. I would have been condemned in spite of all that I had achieved, if I had not sought my army's help" ' (Suetonius, *Julius Caesar* 30). From his own ranks, he says he lost only about 200 killed, 30 of them centurions. Among his dead was Gaius Crastinus, a former *primus pilus* of the Tenth Legion, who had retired but was now serving as a volunteer. 'When the signal was given to engage, he shouted, "Follow me, members of my old century, and give your commander your usual best. There's one battle to go; when it's done, he'll get back his *dignitas* and we our freedom" ' (*The Civil War* III. 91).

The following day, 23,000 of those who had survived the conflict or fled from it surrendered to Caesar. Most of those of senatorial and equestrian rank whom he had already freed before, were put to death, but each of Caesar's friends was allowed to ask for one man to be spared. The rest he added to his complement of officers and other ranks, with instructions that none of them should be victimized. Among the senior officers to whom he gave immunity was Quintus Caepio Brutus, the son of his mistress, Servilia.

CLEOPATRA

# 8

# EGYPTIAN INTERLUDE 48–47 BC

Vain would have been her address
    To the obdurate ears of a jury.
Judged on her looks, not her case,
    With come-hither eyes as her counsel,
Passionately she appealed,
    And a passionate night was the outcome.
                        Lucan, *The Civil War* X. 104–6

Caesar now had much the same dilemma as Pompey had faced after Dyrrachium. He could have returned to Italy in triumph. He could have mopped up the Pompeians who had escaped from Pharsalus. These fugitives, who included Metellus Scipio, Titus Labienus, Lucius Afranius, and Cato, were even now making arrangements to regroup in force in Africa, while Marcus Petreius and Pompey's two sons, Gnaeus and Sextus, were also still at large. Instead, following his private agenda and personal vendetta, Caesar set out to track down Pompey.

It appears, from Cassius Dio, that in Rome those who supported Caesar had cheered whenever there was a military success of any kind, and went around with glum faces when the news was discouraging; fans of Pompey, and those who did not actively support him but detested Caesar, pretended to show the same emotions, for the city teemed with spies and informers. Since reports tended to be conflicting, as the facts would suggest was inevitable, there was ongoing confusion, which became universal consternation when events at Pharsalus unfolded. For such was the nature of the build-up to the battle, and such the apparent inequality of men and resources, that neither party could believe the reports. Matters were not helped in that Caesar diplomatically sent no official dispatch to the government announcing his victory, so as not to appear publicly to be rejoicing at it. Images of Sulla and Pompey were removed from the speakers' platform in the forum, but otherwise people waited to see what would happen.

Caesar sent Mark Antony back to Italy with the legions which he did not immediately need, to look after his interests there. He also appointed Domitius Calvinus, who had commanded his centre at Pharsalus, governor of the province of Asia, and gave him three of Pompey's legions. And it was to Asia that he now went, enjoying, as Alexander the Great had done, the fruits of victory. While passing over his own supposed divine ancestry, Caesar recorded in graphic detail the portents which had been observed in different parts of the Hellenistic world:

> It was established, by going back and calculating the dates, that on the precise day on which Caesar fought his victorious battle, the statue of Victory in front of Minerva in the temple of Minerva at Elis, which had previously faced the image of the goddess, had turned itself round towards the doors and threshold of the temple. And on that same day, cries of an army and the sounds of trumpet calls had twice been heard so loudly at Antioch in Syria, that the citizens armed themselves and ran to and fro on the walls. The same happened at Ptolomais. At Pergamum drums thundered in the sacred and secluded parts of the temple where only priests may go, which the Greeks call 'sanctuaries'. Again, in the temple of Victory at Tralles, where they had dedicated a statue of Caesar, a palm tree was displayed which had at that very time grown out of the stone floor in the joins between the tiles.
>
> *The Civil War* III. 105

What mattered to Caesar was not whether he believed in the significance of such apparent phenomena, but that in people's minds his name and actions were indelibly associated with them.

It was known that Pompey had sailed to Mytilene, on the island of Lesbos, to pick up his wife Cornelia, who had been staying there during the hostilities. Now, he was heard of in Cyprus. Caesar guessed that he was heading for Alexandria, in the hope that the boy king of Egypt, Ptolemy XIII, would place money and resources at his disposal in recognition of the favours Pompey had done to his father. There is also the suggestion that the senate had conferred on Pompey a guardianship over Egypt or Ptolemy XIII, or both. So Caesar set out in pursuit, with two under-strength legions, a squadron of cavalry, and an escort of ten warships. In terms of his time and destiny, it was an expensive error of judgment.

Egyptian politics at this juncture were in a state of turbulence unusual even by the standards of the ancient world. Egypt was ruled by the Hellenistic dynasty of the Ptolemies, founded by Ptolemy I, who was one of the three generals who set themselves up as rulers of Alexander the Great's empire after his death in 323 BC. It had been bequeathed to Rome in 80 BC by Ptolemy XI, who had been established on the throne by Sulla, but was murdered after ruling for only a few weeks. Ptolemy XII Auletes (Fluteplayer) maintained Egypt's independence by paying massive bribes to the senate, and retained his throne by means of additional backhanders to Pompey and Caesar. On his death in 51 BC, he left his kingdom jointly to his daughter Cleopatra VII (born in 69 BC) and his son Ptolemy XIII (born in 61 BC), adjuring the Roman people to ensure that the provisions of his will were observed. In accordance with the protocol that monarchs were living gods and could not marry mortals, Cleopatra married Ptolemy XIII, who was her half-brother. He, as a minor, was advised by his chief ministers, of whom the principal was the eunuch Pothinus.

Neither Cleopatra nor Ptolemy wished to share the throne with anyone else, still less with each other. Cleopatra was driven out of the country. Now she was back, with an army, some 30 miles from the frontier fortress town of Pelusium. Ptolemy XIII, with his home-grown forces, marched out to Pelusium to prevent her entering Egypt. Pompey, who was aiming for Alexandria, somehow learned of these events and altered course so that he could land on the coast near to where Ptolemy and his court were encamped.

Pothinus, Theodotus, the king's tutor, and Achillas, his army commander, considered the implications of this incursion into their plans. If they received Pompey, they would offend Caesar, who would not be far behind, and their private ambitions, and possibly also Egyptian independence, would be jeopardized with the war being brought to their soil. If they rejected him, they would incur Pompey's hatred, and Caesar would give them no thanks for extending his pursuit. If they killed him, however, they would, they thought, incur Caesar's gratitude, and Pompey would no longer be a threat to them. As Theodotus, according to Plutarch, observed with a smile, ' "Dead men don't bite" ' (*Pompey* 72).

And so it was agreed. Since the water was too shallow at that point for Pompey's warship, with its three banks of oars, to land its passengers on the beach, Achillas, with one of Pompey's former officers, set off in a small rowing-boat to fetch him ashore. On the return journey, as they made to land, Pompey was stabbed three times in the back, while Cornelia could only look on from the ship. The date was 28 September 48 BC; Pompey would have been 59 the following day.

A few days later, Caesar sailed into Alexandria, to be presented with Pompey's embalmed head, from which he recoiled in horror. He accepted Pompey's signet ring, however, and is said to have wept over it. Shortly afterwards, lodged in the palace while he tried to recover some of the money which he claimed was still owed to him by Ptolemy Auletes, he received a visitor.

Cleopatra arrived in a sack for storing bedclothes, carried over the shoulder of Apollodorus, a merchant from Sicily, who had brought her by boat along the coast to Alexandria. He untied it in Caesar's presence, and the queen emerged.

While this version of events has elements of melodrama, the fact remains that with Ptolemy's army still blocking the way into Egypt, and the palace out of bounds to Cleopatra, means had to be found to smuggle her back to Alexandria and into the palace itself, without being detected. What followed, however, is the stuff of steamy romance.

Caesar was 52, master of Rome and effectively also of the empire. He had the analytical mind of the complete politician; he was also a consummate ladies' man. Cleopatra, who was there to persuade him to arbitrate in the dispute with her brother, and to arbitrate in her favour, was 21. Whatever happened at that meeting, she got her throne back, and they probably ended up in bed together that same night. The poet Lucan's account would suggest that she was an adorable sex kitten who got her way by flaunting her charms at a susceptible, much older male. It is more likely that Caesar simply saw her as exotic, available, and also highly intelligent. Medieval Arab scholars expressed their admiration not at the way she used her sex appeal to vamp world leaders such as Caesar and subsequently Mark Antony, but at her grasp of astronomy, alchemy, medicine, mathematics, town planning, and philosophy. She also had even then a developed political sense. These facets of her personality, with accompanying conversational skills and her grasp of languages, would have made an immediate impression on a man of Caesar's intellectual capacity as well as on one who appreciated a good lay.

It was probably only after the senate received formal notification of the death of Pompey that Caesar was appointed dictator for a year. He was also awarded a clutch of other honours, including the consulship for five years, the powers of a tribune, authority to decide what should be done about the remaining active supporters of Pompey and to take whatever steps against them he should feel necessary, and indeed to make war against or peace with anyone anywhere on his own initiative. Through his consular colleague for 48 BC, Caesar nominated Mark Antony as master of cavalry, to wield the necessary power in his absence. Mark Antony, now about 35, was still prone to display the roistering instincts of his youth, and the appointment went to his head. He offended the senate, and others, by going about in full military garb, with sword, even when calling the senate to session. He commandeered houses in the city without reimbursement, and, according to Cicero, generally lived it up with unsuitable companions of both sexes.

Meanwhile Caesar, besotted, got himself involved in a local war as well as in a family dispute – or, as he himself put it ingenuously, he was 'by necessity prevented from leaving [Egypt] because of the trade winds, which at that season blow directly against those sailing from Alexandria' (*The Civil War* III. 107). He tried to bring Ptolemy to reason, but the young king, interpreting this approach quite correctly as a sign of favouritism towards his sister, threw a tantrum. There were demonstrations outside the palace. Caesar had to impose his presence by publicly announcing his decision. Cleopatra was reinstated as joint ruler with her brother. A younger sister and brother, Arsinoe and Ptolemy, were to rule jointly the island of Cyprus, the former Egyptian possession which had been annexed to the Roman empire on a technicality in 59 BC. None of this happened. Instead, with Caesar, Cleopatra, Ptolemy XIII, Arsinoe, and the younger Ptolemy uncomfortably ensconced together in the palace, Pothinus ordered Achillas to bring up his forces, take Alexandria, and put the palace under siege.

There were riots in the city, and many of Caesar's soldiers were killed. With the small force still available to him, he fortified the palace environs; he also had access to the harbour, onto which the palace backed. He sent out messengers with frantic but measured calls for reinforcements, both of men and ships, and for supplies. His first tactic was to try and destroy the Egyptian

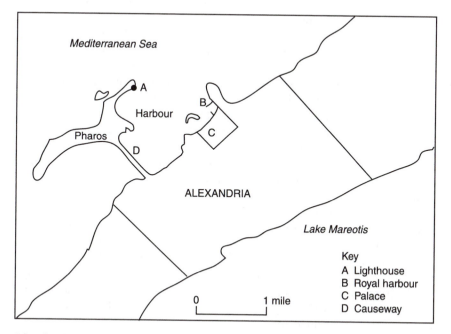

*Plan* 6: Alexandria 48–47 BC

fleet, to free up the approaches to the harbour. In the resulting conflagration a number of storehouses were also destroyed, containing grain and books. Next, to ensure that his ships could pass into and out of the harbour unmolested, he took possession of the Pharos lighthouse at the mouth of the harbour.

Now the teenage Arsinoe, wishing perhaps to have a share of the action if not also of her siblings' throne, slipped out of the palace with her eunuch, Ganymedes, and joined up with Achillas. There was an argument. Achillas was assassinated, and Ganymedes emerged as his successor. Ganymedes now hatched a devilish scheme to replace the fresh water that ran through underground conduits to the palace area with sea water, which he introduced into the system by means of water-wheels. Caesar, to whom civil and military engineering came naturally, countered this ploy by ordering his soldiers to dig wells in the palace grounds. The original trio of plotters were further reduced when Caesar contrived to have Pothinus removed as well.

Caesar's position improved with the arrival of a convoy from Domitius Calvinus with corn, arms, and artillery, as well as the Thirty-Seventh Legion, newly formed from remnants of Pompey's troops who had surrendered. Because of the unfavourable wind, it had to anchor west of Alexandria, but Caesar took ships of his own to fetch the transport vessels in. On the return journey, with only seamen aboard his squadron, he fought a successful battle against an Egyptian fleet, sinking one battleship, capturing another, and killing numerous combat troops. He then sailed into the harbour, towing the heavier supply ships against the breeze.

Caesar was now able to mount a combined naval and military assault on the island of Pharos itself, which was joined to the mainland by a causeway. If successful, he could virtually control the whole harbour. Several battles took place. In one of these, at the southern end of the causeway, Caesar lost 400 legionaries, and found himself in the undignified position of having to jump into the sea and swim for his life. This he did with ease, throwing off his heavy outer garments in the water and holding out of the water in his left hand a number of valuable documents to keep them dry. Suetonius adds that at the same time he dragged his purple military cloak behind him, grasping it between his teeth, to save it falling into Egyptian hands.

It was possibly to divest himself of another potential trouble-maker in the palace that Caesar now bowed to envoys from outside, and allowed them to take Ptolemy XIII back to his supporters. To have a figurehead, not to say also a godhead, among them, however, galvanized the Egyptian army to renewed efforts. Caesar, with only about 3000 troops, was effectively boxed in. He was finally extricated from an embarrassing military, as well as personal, situation in the spring of 47 BC by troops raised in Cilicia and Syria, together with a Jewish army under Antipater, a wealthy Idumaean power-broker. This ad hoc force entered Egypt by way of Ashkelon, and occupied Pelusium. Caesar broke out of the palace environs, his troops now bolstered by the Twenty-Seventh Legion, which he had ordered to follow him from Pharsalus. The Egyptians were trapped between the two forces in the delta of the Nile. Ptolemy drowned, and Arsinoe was captured and sent to Rome.

Caesar was a generous provider, especially to those whose assistance was beyond the calls of duty or, in the case of Cleopatra, of hospitality. He subsequently granted Roman citizenship to Antipater, and appointed him *epitropos* (administrator) of Judaea. Antipater promptly placed two of his sons in responsible positions. Phasael became governor of Jerusalem, and the 25-year-old Herod governor of Galilee. Herod, later known as 'Herod the Great', carved out a career, and a reputation for himself, with Roman assistance, as king of Judaea from 37 to 4 BC. Caesar also passed measures to protect the interests of Jewish communities outside Judaea: they were to be allowed to worship freely, to send contributions to the Temple in Jerusalem, to answer to their own legal system, and to be exempt from conscription into military service.

Caesar could also have taken the opportunity of resolving the local political maelstrom by making Egypt a province of Rome, and thus nominally under the control of the senate. Instead, he rewarded Cleopatra for *her* services by confirming her as queen. Her 11-year-old brother became Ptolemy XIV, and also her new husband. It was now late March. He could have, should have, returned to duty as dictator. There were disturbances in Rome, and discontent elsewhere in Italy. There was serious trouble in Asia Minor, where Pharnaces, king of Bosporus and son of Mithridates, had taken the opportunity of the wars between Caesar and Pompey to try and regain his father's empire. Domitius Calvinus, with one Roman legion and two legions of locals with Roman arms, attempted to oppose him near Nicopolis, but had been heavily defeated. Pharnaces celebrated his victory by occupying Pontus, where he destroyed Amisus, a principal coastal city of the province, selling off the inhabitants into slavery and forcibly castrating all the boys.

Instead, before Caesar said his goodbyes, the unmarried couple, with Cleopatra in an advanced state of pregnancy, took a two-month honeymoon on the Nile: 'They often feasted through the night until dawn, and would have sailed in the royal yacht right through Egypt almost as far as Ethiopia, if his soldiers had not declined to accompany them' (Suetonius, *Julius Caesar* 52).

As a going-away present, Caesar gave Cleopatra Cyprus, and to help her maintain internal order left with her three legions which he could ill afford to spare. Then, at the beginning of June, he sailed on the first stage of the long journey home, with a much depleted Sixth Legion, which had served him loyally in Gaul, in Spain, at Pharsalus, and now in Alexandria. On the way, he would see what could be done about Pharnaces.

A few weeks later, on 23 June according to an inscription on a gravestone which refers to it as the birthday of 'King Caesar', Cleopatra had a son. His official names were Ptolemy Caesar, but the Alexandrians, and history, took

*Figure 8.1* Early first-century AD head of Caesar, with receding hairline, from Egypt, carved in green slate, in Berlin Museum. (C. M. Dixon/ Ancient Art & Architecture Collection)

to calling him Caesarion (Little Caesar). Cleopatra always claimed that he was Caesar's, but then she would, wouldn't she? For the heir to the throne of the Ptolemies was thus Roman as well as Egyptian, and ruled jointly with her as Ptolemy Caesar after the untimely death of Ptolemy XIV in 44 BC – it is said that Cleopatra poisoned him. And Caesarion was not only Roman; he was the son of the most powerful Roman of all. Caesar never denied that he was the father, and, according to Suetonius, Mark Antony informed the senate that he had openly admitted paternity to reliable acquaintances. Caesar had nothing material to lose by doing this. He could not marry Cleopatra because she was not Roman; nor, for the same reason, could Caesarion inherit from him. Also, Caesar had been married three times for a total of over 30 years, and had had numerous mistresses, without ever fathering a son: just one daughter, and she after about 10 years of marriage. To have had a son, at the age of 53, with the queen of the east, so soon after first meeting her, was something to boast about to one's male friends.

One man's boast, however, is often the cause of other people's doubts. It is regarded as medically improbable that Caesar could have fathered a son with Cleopatra so soon, and after so many years of apparent sterility. Further, Caesar arrived in Alexandria in early October 48 BC, by the Roman calendar then in force, when Cleopatra was some 250 miles away. It is hardly likely that she could have organized her arduous and hazardous journey to arrive to meet him much before the end of the month. Even if Cleopatra conceived at her first encounter with Caesar, a baby born to them on 23 June 47 by the old Roman calendar would be several weeks premature. Such a baby, the first child of a 22-year-old from a family steeped in incest, who was herself the daughter of a brother and sister, would in those times have stood little chance of a normal survival, yet there is no suggestion that Caesarion was an unhealthy infant. But if Caesar was not the father, then who was? Certainly not Cleopatra's brother, and husband, Ptolemy XIII, who was away making war against her at the time. A fleeting affair, abandoned when Caesar came on the scene, or a one-night stand seem as implausible as they are improbable. Certainly, Caesar's principal heir, his great-nephew Octavius, believed the claim sufficiently to have Caesarion eliminated when he was about 17. At best, however, the verdict in Scottish law of 'not proven' would seem to be the most applicable in the case of Caesar's paternity; and Scottish law, unlike English law, derives from Roman law.

On his journey from Alexandria, Caesar stopped off first at Antioch, where he spent several days attending to the affairs of the province of Syria and its satellite states. From there he went to Tarsus, to which he summoned all the significant citizens of Cilicia. He also gave audiences and granted amnesties to several former associates of Pompey, including Gaius Cassius Longinus, who was serving as a naval commander in 48 BC and had not been present at Pharsalus. The meeting with Caesar was arranged by Caepio Brutus, who was Cassius's brother-in-law; for Cassius had married Tertia, daughter of Servilia and rumoured at one time to have been another of Caesar's mistresses.

Now Caesar was ready to take on Pharnaces. As he approached Galatia, he was met by Deiotarus, who had, on Pompey's orders, been appointed king of Armenia Minor as well as being tetrarch of Galatia, wearing the garb of a suppliant. Deiotarus apologized profusely for having supported Pompey in the recent war, and asked to be pardoned. Caesar was not in such a forgiving mood on this occasion. He particularly reminded Deiotarus that he, not Pompey, was at the time designated by the senate head of state. He allowed him, however, to retain the title of king, but demanded the loan of his legion, raised and trained locally but with Roman arms and equipment, and all his cavalry. With these, two legions borrowed from Domitius Calvinus, and the faithful Sixth, now down to only about a thousand men, he marched towards Zela, where Pharnaces was encamped.

With 20 miles to go, he was met by envoys from Pharnaces. They bore a circlet of gold, and offered him Pharnaces's daughter in marriage. Caesar diplomatically rejected this somewhat naive proposal, and advanced to within 5 miles of Pharnaces, where on 1 August he made camp. Zela stood proudly on a plain, surrounded by hills intersected by steep ravines. Pharnaces occupied one of the more strategic of these hills. During the night, Caesar moved forward with his legions in light order, and took the hill facing Pharnaces. The two armies were now only about a mile apart, with between them a ravine which Caesar reckoned would give him as much protection as it did Pharnaces.

The battle of Zela is one of the more extraordinary in the history of the ancient world. At dawn, while Caesar's men were digging in, Pharnaces drew up his army, and descended into the ravine, from where he made a surprise uphill assault on the Roman position. An astonished Caesar ordered his men to exchange their trenching tools for their weapons and to form up in defensive lines. They forced the enemy back into the ravine, and there slaughtered them. Four hours later, with his entire army either dead or captured, Pharnaces fled on horseback to Sinope. This encounter inspired Caesar's aphorism, 'Veni, vidi, vici (I came, I saw, I conquered).'

Caesar gave over all Pharnaces's valuables as booty for his troops. Having tidied up military and political affairs in the region, he returned to Italy by sea, leaving an elated Sixth Legion to make its own way home. He landed at Tarentum in late September, as usual before anyone expected him. From there, instead of travelling straight to Rome, he went by road to Brundisium, where an anxious Cicero was to meet him. Though Cicero was not at the battle of Pharsalus, he was still in Greece at the time. After it, he had nowhere to go except back to Italy. He landed at Brundisium, but got no farther. A message came from Mark Antony, who hated Cicero for his treatment of his stepfather Lentulus over the Catiline affair. Caesar had given orders in writing that no supporter of Pompey's cause was to be allowed back into Italy without his express permission. Until Caesar returned to Italy, Cicero must remain where he was.

Cicero waited for Caesar by the roadside a little way from the town, with other local dignitaries behind him. When Caesar saw Cicero, he jumped down from his carriage, and embraced him. They then, as they walked together, had a private conversation, the upshot of which seems to have been that Cicero was free to go where and when he liked.

ANTONY

# 9

# THE DICTATOR
## Civil War 47–45 BC

Cicero said that he perceived a despotic intention in most of
Caesar's schemes and political acts. 'On the other hand,' he
maintained, 'when I look at him, with his hair so neatly
combed, gently scratching his head with one finger, it never
occurs to me that such a man would ever entertain such a
heinous crime as to destroy the Roman republic.'

Plutarch, *Caesar* 4

The *clementia* (clemency) that Caesar showed to his opponents should not be
confused, for instance, with *humanitas* (humanity) or *mansuetudo* (gentleness),
other terms which were bandied about in this context. It was primarily
motivated by political considerations. The aphorism, 'When you forgive an
enemy you win several friends at no cost', must have been known to him, for
it is attributed to the mime-writer Publilius Syrus, whom Caesar invited to
perform at his games in 46 BC. Caesar certainly acted upon it, and it stood
him in particularly good stead when he returned to Rome in 47 BC, and
could now rely on the moral support of the nobility. During the previous
11 years and 9 calendar months, he had been in Rome for a total of 25 days at

most. It was two years since he had seen his wife, or, for that matter, Servilia, and rumours of his Egyptian fling, which would have been rife in Rome, must have affected them both. Not that he had ever been particularly faithful to either of them, but he did not normally evince such blatant indiscretion.

His priority was not, however, political or personal affairs at home, but military issues in Africa, where the beneficiaries of his *clementia* had raised ten new legions. Juba, still nursing his implacable hatred of Caesar, contributed a further four Numidian legions, trained in the Roman style of warfare. There was also a complement of 15,000 cavalry. Metellus Scipio, possibly out of respect to his late son-in-law Pompey, was elected commander-in-chief, with the vastly experienced Labienus as his second-in-command. Attacks by sea had been made on coastal cities of Sardinia and Sicily, and great quantities of arms and other iron implements had been looted. There were rumours of a planned two-pronged invasion of Italy, by sea from Africa and by land from Spain, where Gnaeus Pompeius Magnus was ensconced with further legions loyal to his father's cause.

Nevertheless, there were still problems at home to be dealt with first. No consular elections had been held for 47 BC. Caesar rewarded his loyal lieutenants Publius Vatinius and Fufius Calenus, who as tribune had assisted Clodius in 61 BC and subsequently served as a legate, by having them elected consuls for what remained of the year. He made other significant appointments, including the elevation to the priesthood in place of Domitius Ahenobarbus, who had been killed at Pharsalus, of his great-nephew Octavius, who had just turned 16.

Elections had been held, however, in Caesar's absence for the posts of tribune of the people. Cicero's unsatisfactory son-in-law, Cornelius Dolabella, had used the same route to one of the posts as had Clodius, by having himself adopted into a plebeian family. Once in office, he had campaigned energetically and violently for the cancellation of debts, with which he was himself overburdened, and also rents. His supporters occupied the forum, which they surrounded with wooden barricades. Mark Antony, as master of the cavalry, was granted a *senatus consultum ultimum* to use troops against them. In the resulting fracas, several hundred Roman citizens were killed, the tablets on which Dolabella had inscribed his measures were smashed, and a number of protesters were hurled from the Tarpeian rock on the summit of the Capitol Hill, a punishment usually reserved for murderers and traitors. As a result of this overreaction to the situation, Antony lost the confidence of the senate, the people, and also, for the time being, Caesar. With Caesar's official term of office as dictator now having expired, Antony was out of a job. In spite of his experience as an army officer, and his loyalty to Caesar, he was not appointed to any command in the forthcoming African campaign.

Dolabella, however, was treated with indulgence, and his measures with a modicum of respect; he was also invited to accompany Caesar to Africa. According to Cassius Dio, Caesar now cancelled all interest on debts owing since the beginning of hostilities, though not the debts themselves. After all, he explained, he too was dependent on loans, now that he had spent all his private means in the public good. He did not add that these 'loans' were monies and other valuables that he had confiscated from cities and private individuals. He did, on the other hand, take notice of the unrest about rents, and authorized the cancellation of these for a year, up to a certain limit.

The properties of opponents in the conflict who had died or who had forfeited Caesar's good will were publicly auctioned. Mark Antony, however, was furious at being made to pay the full price he had bid for Pompey's house. Servilia, on the other hand, picked up several bargains at prices manipulated by Caesar.

The African campaign might never have begun had not Caesar personally intervened in an ugly incident of mutiny. The veteran legions which had recently marched back from Pharsalus were now being mustered in Campania ready to embark, in winter, for Africa, to fight an enemy whom they understood they had already defeated. They demanded their discharge and the final bonus that they claimed they were due. Peace brokers were greeted with showers of stones. Caesar sent a special negotiator, the praetor Gaius Sallustius Crispus (the historian Sallust), with a promise of an additional thousand *denarii* to each soldier. The men replied that they wanted cash, not promises, and Sallust was lucky to get away with his life as they moved off in a body to take their grievances to Rome itself. Two senators whom they encountered en route were unceremoniously killed. When the mutineers reached the Campus Martius, outside the city limits, they encamped and awaited developments.

Caesar considered using the special forces at his disposal, but decided that the risk was too great that these might join the mutiny, and in any case he was loath to lose any of his valuable fighting men in a clash with the forces of the law. Instead, without giving them any warning, he walked alone into the mutineers' camp and mounted a platform. From there, he listened patiently to their complaints and demands. Then he addressed them: 'Citizens,' he began, thus diplomatically but firmly indicating that they had been dismissed from the army. He went on to say that he fully sympathized with their situation, and that when he returned from Africa they would receive all that was due to them in bonuses, severance pay, and land grants. The troops needed Caesar as much as Caesar needed his troops, and to a man they begged to be re-enlisted.

Caesar pretended to think it over. Then, with a show of reluctance, he agreed, except in the case of the Tenth Legion, who had been through so much with him and had regularly been given the position of honour in battle. The soldiers of the Tenth were stunned. Their representatives asked that the legion should be decimated rather than dismissed. Caesar, reckoning that he had now screwed out of the mutineers enough assurances of loyalty and obedience, took them, too, back into service. Being inflexible, however, where military discipline was concerned, he saw to it that for the remainder of his campaign the Tenth was always sent into the most lethal situations.

Before finally leaving for Africa, Caesar ensured continuity of government by having himself and the loyal Lepidus elected consuls for 46 BC, increasing the number of praetors and priests to accommodate some of his supporters, and appointing to the senate, as replacements for those who had died, equestrians and others who had served him well as army officers. He now embarked for Africa at Lilybaeum, the western point of Sicily, without waiting for the recently re-enlisted veterans to arrive. At this stage he had five legions of recruits, the experienced Fifth (*Alaudae*), which had probably not been on his recent eastern campaign, and 2000 cavalry. Surprise, he reckoned, was going to weigh more heavily than mere numbers.

The crossing was chaotic even considering the time of year. Caesar finally put in at Hadrumetum at the end of December 47 BC with only 3000 troops and 150 cavalry, the rest having been carried away by the winds. Just as he set foot on land, he tripped and fell flat on his face. Onlookers were aghast at this most inauspicious of omens – it also appears, from a remark of Cicero, that Caesar had embarked on this expedition against the advice of his senior augur. With great presence of mind, however, he stretched out his arms, grasped the ground, kissed it, and exclaimed, ' "Ha! I've got you, Africa" ' (Cassius Dio, *Roman History* XLII. 58).

Without a viable force, Caesar deputed Publius Vatinius to look for the lost ships, sent what transports he had back to Sicily to pick up more troops, and ordered Sallust to sail south and take the island of Cercina in the gulf of the Lesser Syrtis, where he had had intelligence that the enemy had stored quantities of grain. It was, however, Caesar who received the first surprise. After camping north of Leptis Minor, where he was joined by the missing transports, he led out 30 cohorts to requisition supplies. Clouds of dust confirmed the reports of his scouts that a considerable enemy force was approaching. He sent orders to the camp for his 150 archers and all available cavalry to be sent up to join him, while he himself went forward with a small reconnaissance party.

When the two sides lined up on the open plain, Caesar realized that the opposition, under the leadership of Labienus, comprised massed cavalry supported not by infantry, as he had supposed, but close-packed light-armed auxiliaries and unmounted archers, whose line of battle extended much farther than his. Superlative tactics on his part enabled his much smaller and weaker force to take the initiative, and he was engaged in ordering a tactical withdrawal when Petreius appeared at the head of 1600 cavalry, 6000 heavy and light infantry, numerous archers, mounted and on foot, and slingers. It was not until sundown that Caesar was able to extricate what was left of his force from the conflict, which at one point was going so badly for him that some of his men panicked and began to run away from the field. Caesar caught hold of a standard-bearer, forcibly turned him about, and shouted at him and his fellow fugitives, ' "That way, the enemy" ' (Plutarch, *Caesar* 52).

The full hostilities, which lasted for three months, were only notable for the tactical manoeuvring of both sides. Caesar's problems with supplies were eased by a successful raid by Sallust on Cercina, and with manpower by the arrival of the Thirteenth and Fourteenth legions, which had served under him in Gaul, and subsequently of the veterans of the Ninth and Tenth. Metellus Scipio's difficulties were compounded when Bocchus, whom Caesar had formally recognized in 49 BC as joint king of Mauretania with his brother Bogud, invaded Numidia, causing Juba temporarily to abandon the proceedings to defend his own territory. Meanwhile both sides mounted propaganda campaigns, by means of pamphlets and word of mouth, aimed at subverting each other's troops. Caesar's was much the more successful: he promised to safeguard the possessions of locally enlisted troops, and to pardon all Roman troops and pay them the same bounties he was offering to his own men.

The final showdown came at Thapsus. By a combined land and sea operation, Caesar managed to draw Scipio into deploying his army in battle formation, with a squadron of Juba's elephants on each wing. Caesar's plan was to draw up his troops in three lines as at Pharsalus, with detachments of the Fifth Legion, who had demanded this privilege, behind each wing in oblique formation to deal with the elephants. He was still arranging the disposition of his forces when someone trumpeted the charge. At this, his lines ran against the enemy, shouldering aside their own centurions who tried to stand in their way. Caesar, seeing that there was nothing more he could do about it, had his own trumpeter sound the 'Good luck' signal, gave his horse his head, and galloped at the enemy front rank. In the chaos, Scipio's elephants ran amok and trampled to death many of their own troops. The survivors fled. Ten thousand of them, including many of their officers, surrendered en masse, only to be butchered as Caesar's soldiers gave vent to their pent-up frustration, while Caesar himself could only look on, appalled.

There was frustration, too, on the part of Scipio's cavalry which had escaped from the battle. Finding their way barred into Utica, which was administered by Cato, they forced the gates, massacred many of the inhabitants, and looted buildings. Cato had to bribe them out of his own pocket to go away. Then, rather than give Caesar the satisfaction of pardoning him, which he claimed that Caesar did not have the right to do, having no legitimate authority over him, he arranged his personal and civic affairs, and killed himself, with the utmost dignity if rather messily. His death marked the end of constructive republicanism, if not yet also of the republic itself.

Caesar's other principal opponents met mixed fortunes. Labienus and Sextus Pompeius, younger brother of Gnaeus, made it to Spain. That Metellus Scipio and Afranius did not do so was due to the alertness of Publius Sittius, by the standards of the ancient world an elderly, but still very energetic, member of the equestrian class. Wealthy and influential, he was a friend of

Sulla and more recently of Cicero. After being suspected of complicity in the activities of Catiline, he sold off his properties and interests in Italy and hired himself out to the kingdom of Mauretania as a naval and military mercenary commander. The warships carrying Scipio and his escort to Spain were intercepted by Sittius's fleet off the coast of Numidia, and sunk. Afranius, who was trying to reach Spain overland with 1000 survivors, was ambushed, captured, and executed.

Juba, with Petreius, rode hot foot to his royal city of Zama, whose inhabitants, having heard of Caesar's victory, flatly refused them entry. With Caesar, escorted by Juba's cavalry, which had surrendered to him and been pardoned, now approaching Zama, Juba and Petreius retired to one of the royal country houses. There, they dined together, before fighting a sword duel to the death. Juba killed his former ally, and then ordered a slave to do the same for him.

With the rank and file, Caesar followed his predetermined policy. First-time offenders were granted amnesty: those who had been pardoned before were executed. Civilians and whole communities which had supported the Pompeian cause were heavily fined. He established colonies along the coast of the province of Africa in which he settled potential trouble-makers from his army, before sailing for Sardinia. Here, besides imposing huge fines and increased taxes, he weeded out further troublesome elements from the ranks of his army and dispatched them as reinforcements to Spain, where now both sons of Pompey were keeping alive their father's memory. To the Fifth Legion he awarded the unique accolade of an elephant as its permanent emblem.

Caesar returned to Rome on 26 May 46 BC, having spent 27 days on the sea journey from Carales on the south coast of Sardinia – Roman seafarers avoided the open sea wherever possible, preferring to hug the shoreline, and bad weather had constantly bottled him up in ports along the way. His arrival was the signal for unprecedented jubilation and a flood of honours. Forty days of thanksgiving were decreed for his victory. He was granted a ten-day, fourfold triumph for defeating Gaul, the Egyptians, Pharnaces, and Juba – diplomatically, there was no mention in this context of his victories at Pharsalus and Thapsus. He was elected dictator for ten years, 'rei publicae constituendae (to put the constitution in order)', and given the title and office for three years of 'Controller of Public Morals'. He had the authority to appoint officials of state, and the right to sit in the senate on a curule chair beside the consuls and to speak first on any issue. A bronze statue of him astride the known world was commissioned, with an inscription to the effect that he was a demigod – he allowed the image to go ahead, but had the legend discreetly erased.

Caesar responded with a speech in the senate in which he assured the general public that he had no intention of being a Marius, or a Cinna, or a Sulla, who began their rules, after triumphing over their enemies, by acting benevolently in order to attract popular support, and then did the opposite. He would be their champion, their leader, not a tyrant. The army was there to benefit the public and the empire, not to be a tool of oppression. Inevitably, its upkeep had involved higher taxes, but he himself had reaped no personal benefit from these, having spent in the public good all his own capital and much that he had borrowed. On the contrary, part of the increase went towards the wars, and the rest was safe, and would be spent on adorning the city and on sound administration.

The triumphal processions, one on each of four days, began with the worst of omens. The axle of Caesar's chariot broke as it was passing the temple of Fortune, depositing him in the road. While waiting for a replacement, he demonstrated his humility by climbing up the steps of the Capitoline temple on his knees.

The crowds had a great time. They saw Arsinoe led in chains behind Caesar's chariot. She was afterwards released, only to be killed later, at Cleopatra's insistence and on the orders of Mark Antony, in the temple at Ephesus where she had obtained sanctuary. Also released after marching in the procession was Juba, four-year-old son of the late king of Numidia. He was then brought up in Italy and granted Roman citizenship; subsequently he was reinstated on the throne of Numidia, married a daughter of Mark Antony and Cleopatra, and became a much respected scholar and author of learned treatises. Other prisoners-of-war, including Vercingetorix, were less fortunate. Having served their purpose, they were taken away and strangled.

To mark the Gallic triumph, the veteran legions who had served in Gaul paraded past, happily chanting rude marching songs:

> Caesar celebrates a triumph:
>   Nicomedes bugger all!
> Nicomedes buggered Caesar;
>   Caesar buggered Gaul!
>
> Suetonius, *Julius Caesar* 49

> Lock up your wives, inhabitants of Rome,
>   His army brings the bald adulterer home.
> The gold he borrowed for his Gallic wars,
>   He spent instead upon his Gallic whores.
>
> Suetonius, *Julius Caesar* 51

Caesar took all this in good part – except for the references to Nicomedes. Cassius Dio records that he protested on oath that he had done nothing wrong, which only made matters worse!

What also amazed the crowds was the amount of booty in the form of coin and bullion which was dragged past in ox-wagons. This was afterwards distributed not only as prize money to the troops (each legionary received roughly the equivalent of 20 years' pay), but also as bonuses to 320,000 needy citizens, who in addition were given free supplies of corn and oil.

To honour an undertaking made when his daughter Julia died, Caesar gave a public feast at which 22,000 tables were laid, groaning with food; the catering was done partly by his personal staff and partly by contractors. Afterwards he was escorted home by elephants carrying torches, and by what seemed to be the whole populace. Then there were the games, for days on end, staged mainly in an up-to-date form of wooden venue which he designed, with seats all round, known as an amphitheatre. Gladiators fought to the death, actors performed on mobile stages, and athletes ran and wrestled against each other. There was a big game hunt which went on for five days, during which 400 lions were slaughtered and 40 elephants were goaded by their riders to fight each other. There were sea battles on an artificial lake dug out of the Campus Martius, and a land battle between two armies of condemned criminals and prisoners-of-war. And as a special attraction, the public of Rome were treated for the first time to the sight of a giraffe, which they called a cameleopard.

Not everyone appreciated Caesar's lavishness. Some of his veterans felt that part of the money might have been better spent as additional bonuses for them. To put a stop once and for all to potential mutinies, Caesar went up to one of the protesters, grabbed him, and led him off to instant execution. Two others were ordered to be publicly sacrificed and their heads strung up outside his official residence as *pontifex maximus*. This deliberate and brutal application of religious ritual to a breach of military discipline would have made, as it was intended to, a particular impression on the public, since human sacrifice was not a Roman practice.

Caesar also set himself a massive programme of political and administrative reforms, while continuing to demonstrate a merciful attitude to former opponents, especially those of noble upbringing. Such a one was the rabid republican Marcus Marcellus, consul in 51 BC and flogger of the colonial senator, who had gone into voluntary exile in Mytilene after Pompey's defeat at Pharsalus. His property was still untouched, and when, following a proposal by Calpurnius Piso, Marcus's cousin Gaius Marcellus (husband of Octavia) pleaded for him on his knees in the senate, Caesar agreed that he should return. On his way back, however, Marcus was murdered in Athens by a friend whom Cicero understood to be temporarily deranged.

Caesar's style was autocratic because that was what he felt the situation demanded, as even Cicero initially conceded. His task had been given to him; he had not asked for it. Only someone of considerable political insight and ability could have responded to the challenge, especially if it is taken into account that for the last 12 years he had been primarily concerned with waging war, winning military battles in the field, and protecting his own back from adversarial elements at home. He did not consult other senators; he raised issues among his inner circle of friends, Cornelius Balbus, Gaius Oppius, Gaius Matius, Aulus Hirtius, Gaius Vibius Pansa. A small army of clerks stood by to draft edicts, decrees, or laws, as the constitution demanded.

*Figure 9.1* Marble bust of Caesar from the Vatican Museums, Rome, believed to be a late first-century BC or early first-century AD copy of a bronze done in his lifetime. (Prisma/Ancient Art & Architecture Collection)

He informed the senate when it suited him to do so, whether it was presenting for official ratification matters which had already been decided, or requesting action along lines which he had already mapped out. Otherwise, when necessary, he simply used the names of prominent senators as supporters of a bill without their knowledge. Cicero was amused to receive letters from foreign kings of whose existence he was unaware, thanking him for proposing them for their royal title.

In the same way as he tackled the crucial question of debts without putting too much pressure on the creditors, so, in resolving the distribution of land to army veterans, Caesar was careful not to antagonize existing landowners.

In the first place, settlements were arranged by his own officers, not by a senatorial committee. Then, wherever possible, the distributions were of public land, or land for which compensation had been given or which had been confiscated from unrepentant supporters of Pompey. Where land had to be appropriated compulsorily, there was machinery whereby the landowner could obtain redress for unfair treatment. Initially, care was taken to spread the new occupants over as wide a geographical area as possible, and to avoid enmity by settling them apart from hereditary landowners. As a long-term project, Caesar planned also to create more public land by draining the Pomptine Marshes and Lake Fucinus.

Maybe 20,000 other veterans of his wars, along with 60,000 or more Roman citizens of indeterminate resources, were settled in overseas colonies which Caesar founded or instigated in southern Gaul, Sardinia, Spain, north Africa, Greece, and Asia Minor. It was significant that in these Roman establishments, a slave who had obtained his freedom could hold the office of municipal councillor. Land was cheaper overseas, but also the existence throughout the empire of a growing number of pockets of Roman, as opposed to Romanized, society further undermined the influence which under the republic could be exercised through their clientele by a few powerful individuals. The process was boosted by Caesar's policy of enfranchisement. He granted citizenship to all doctors and teachers of liberal arts practising in Rome, and to individuals, regions, and groups in the provinces of the empire, including the whole complement of the Fifth Legion (*Alaudae*), which had been raised in Transalpine Gaul. Communities which were still of predominantly native stock received Latin rights.

The composition of the senate was changed out of all recognition, not simply by his ultimately increasing its numbers from 600 to 900, but through making the nominal centre of government into more of a people's parliament by admitting members from the provinces and from Italian communities, as well as soldiers and the sons of freedmen, all owing their appointments to him. Partly, no doubt, to reward those who had given him particular personal support, he further increased the number of praetors, appointed additional aediles, and doubled the number of quaestors. Maybe it was to obviate the need for tiresome elections that he appointed city prefects to do the work of senior elected officials. It was certainly to lessen the chance of opposition factions being fostered abroad that he limited the governorships of ex-consuls to two years, and of ex-praetors to one year. He also introduced a fast-track system whereby a man could be appointed to a particular rank without having served at a lower level.

It seems that very little escaped his eagle eye for measures which would improve social and economic conditions. He held a census and reduced the number of those who received the corn dole – many of those no longer entitled would be among the new colonials. He revised the composition of juries. There were to be restrictions on the purchase of some luxury goods and on extravagant spending. To compensate for the loss of lives during the civil wars, which all told were estimated by polymath Pliny the Elder (AD 23/4–79) to have been 1,192,000, he undertook to reward those with large families. To meet the educational and scholarly needs of the new, and old, citizens, Caesar invited Marcus Terentius Varro to plan and organize the first ever public library in Rome. To ensure the streets were more passable and safer, he introduced traffic regulations and banned political clubs masquerading as guilds: genuine, long-established trade associations and assemblies of Jews were specifically excluded.

Of lasting significance was Caesar's reform of the calendar, which had been based on the lunar year and had got into such a tangle during the civil war that mid-summer fell in September. With the help of Sosigenes, Cleopatra's astronomer, he devised and put into immediate practice a new calendar based on the solar year, similar to that which operated in Egypt, but with modifications. The seasons of the agricultural year were now reconciled with the revolution of the moon round the earth, while what were traditionally the special days in the month were disturbed as little as possible. He also put a stop to the traditional right of the priests to insert days and months on their own initiative, or in response to the personal demands of state officials and those eligible to collect taxes, to whom a longer or shorter year could be advantageous as the case might be. In this respect the reform of the calendar was an act executed by Caesar in his capacity as dictator rather than *pontifex maximus*. However it is regarded, it was a brilliant performance on the part of someone who was fully able to grasp issues on the boundaries of astronomical science, which, apart from a small adjustment by Pope Gregory XIII in the sixteenth century, has never been improved upon.

The Roman lunar year consisted of 355 days. The Egyptians had 12 months of 30 days each, and made up their year by adding an extra five days at its end. Caesar arrived at his year of precisely 365¼ days by distributing these five days, plus two that he deducted from February, among seven months; he made up the whole day which accrued from the accumulation of quarters by adding it to February every fourth year. In acknowledgement of his contribution, the month in which his birthday fell, the fifth month of the original calendar, which until 153 BC began in March, was later called July in his honour. In order that the new Julian calendar could be implemented on 1 January 45 BC, Caesar allowed for the statutory intercalary month of 23 days at the end of February, and inserted two extra months of 33 and 34 days between November and December 46 BC. Astronomical phenomena could now be predicted. Cicero was not impressed. When someone observed to him that the constellation of Lyra would rise the following night, he joked, ' "Indeed, and by dictatorial decree" ' (Plutarch, *Caesar* 59).

While all this frantic public business was being conducted, Cleopatra arrived in Rome for an extended state visit, accompanied by her 12-year-old husband and her one-year-old son. Caesar was charmed, and put them up in his secluded villa in the gardens on the other side of the river Tiber. Roman society was scandalized. Caesar took no notice, and formally enrolled the royal couple as friends and allies of the Roman people. Calpurnia's views are not recorded.

There was also the matter of the statue. Caesar's extension to the forum, the Forum Julium, had been in use since 54 BC. It now also contained the temple of Venus Genetrix, dedicated by Caesar to Venus as mother of Aeneas, mythological founder of Rome, and as divine ancestor of the Julii. To decorate the interior, Caesar bought, for almost two million sesterces, two mythological paintings, by Timomachus of Byzantium, of Ajax and Medea. Beside the cult-statue of Venus herself, he now placed a 'beautiful image of Cleopatra' (Appian, *Civil Wars* II. 102).

To install a statue of one's foreign mistress in the holiest position in a temple was, on the face of it, an act not only of supreme arrogance and insensitivity, but also of impiety, especially on the part of the head of the religion of the state, even if he was at the time also supreme ruler. Was it actually commissioned by Caesar, or did Cleopatra perhaps bring it with her from Egypt as a gift to him in his capacity as Roman head of state? She was perfectly capable of deliberately cocking such a snook at Roman society, but might the statue also have carried some deeper implication? The worship of the Egyptian mother goddess Isis had been practised in Rome by some folk alongside the religion of the state since the beginning of the first century BC, though it was officially frowned upon. Cleopatra was in Egypt identified as Isis, and is represented as Isis–Aphrodite on coins of the time issued in Cyprus. In literary tradition the Greek goddess Aphrodite was closely associated with Cyprus; her equivalent in Roman mythology is Venus. If the statue represented Cleopatra as the mother goddess Isis, or as Isis–Aphrodite, then Caesar's location of the gift, beside the goddess mother of the Julii, though unprecedented in republican Rome, was at least of genuine religious significance. That this is a valid hypothesis is suggested by the fact that, again according to Appian, Cleopatra's statue was still there, in the temple of Venus Genetrix, 200 years later, in spite of her having in the meantime been declared an enemy of Rome.

Caesar was also anxious to get back to Spain, where his nominee as governor, Gaius Trebonius, had taken over Pompey's job, only to be sent packing by Pompey's elder son Gnaeus. Caesar's two generals in Spain, his nephew Quintus Pedius and Quintus Fabius Maximus, whose troops were mainly untried, were unable to contain the opposition, which, now that it had been boosted by the arrival of Sextus Pompeius, Labienus, and what remained of their African troops, numbered 13 legions. They had therefore encamped near Corduba, to await developments. The situation called for the personal intervention of Caesar, which he engineered with his usual flair, élan, and disregard for constitutional niceties.

Lepidus, as Caesar's consular colleague for the year, was put nominally in charge of affairs in Rome, with eight prefects to assist him, though the real authority was vested in Balbus and Oppius. Then, having hastily called up the available troops, Caesar set out for Spain, leaving behind Octavius, who was too ill to accompany his great-uncle on campaign. Caesar must have travelled by closed carriage, because he arrived on the scene before either the opposition or even his own men knew he was on the way, having covered 1500 miles in 27 days, during which he whiled away the time by writing a narrative poem, 'The Journey'. He was well ahead of his additional legions. These included the experienced Fifth, and also the Sixth and Tenth, which had been disbanded after Zela and Thapsus respectively, and were now brought back into service with, as their core, former soldiers of these legions who had been settled in Arelate and Narbo, on Caesar's route to Spain. After Caesar's departure from Rome, Lepidus appointed himself master of the cavalry, in which capacity he went through the process of instigating consular elections, at which Caesar was designated sole consul for 45 BC.

Caesar's Spanish campaign, fought in the south during the winter, was hard and bloody. While Sextus Pompeius held Corduba, the chief centre of Romanized life in Spain, his brother Gnaeus was besieging Ulia, a town which had always been staunchly pro-Roman. In order to draw Gnaeus off from Ulia, and maybe even commit him to battle, Caesar marched in the direction of Corduba, sending ahead several cohorts of heavy infantry accompanied by cavalry leading spare horses. As they approached the town, the infantrymen mounted the spare horses, to give the impression that the detachment consisted entirely of cavalry without protection. Sextus sent out a considerable force from the town, expecting to cut the cavalry to pieces. Caesar's infantrymen dismounted, formed up in battle array, and disposed of the opposition so conclusively that Sextus sent a dispatch to his brother asking for his help. Gnaeus, duly disturbed, abandoned the siege of Ulia and marched north.

Caesar reached the immediate surroundings of Corduba first, having crossed the river Baetis with his army on a makeshift bridge of planks supported on wicker baskets filled with stones and sunk into the running stream. There followed over the next few days a series of inconclusive running battles between detachments of the two sides, conducted in appalling conditions with much carnage. Finally, at the beginning of January 45 BC, Caesar withdrew his troops to concentrate on taking the fortified town of Ategua, about 20 miles to the south-east, where there were large stocks of grain. In spite of the skill and ingenuity of Caesar's engineers, the Pompeian troops inside the town held out until 19 February, even making damaging sorties against the besiegers, in the course of an engagement marked by brutality on both sides. Two Spanish legionaries, captured by Caesar's cavalry, claimed that they were slaves. When they were brought in, they were recognised as having been originally in the service of Trebonius, and were immediately executed as traitors. A party of couriers, bringing dispatches from Corduba to Gnaeus Pompius, ended up by mistake in Caesar's camp. They were sent on their way with their hands cut off. In Ategua itself, the troops massacred civilians whom they suspected of being sympathetic to the cause of Caesar and flung their bodies down from the walls.

Gnaeus was finally brought to battle at Munda. His army included two Spanish legions which had come over to him from Gaius Trebonius, one raised locally from Roman settlers, one originally commanded by Afranius in Africa, and nine others of unproven reliability; these were supported by 12,000 light-armed troops and auxiliary infantry, and several detachments of cavalry. Caesar had eight legions and 8000 cavalry. Among the latter was a squadron of Numidians commanded by Bogud, king of Mauretania, with whose wife Eunoe Caesar had had, or was at the time having, an affair – it is said that he rewarded Bogud handsomely for the experience.

At the height of the battle, the unthinkable happened. With the two sides locked together and bent on cutting each other down, Caesar's veteran legions began to give way, until a gap appeared between the two opposing armies. Caesar jumped from his horse, threw off his helmet to ensure that his men recognized him, grabbed a shield, and ran to the front of his own line, shouting to anyone who could hear, ' "This is the end of me, *and* your army service" ' (Appian, *Civil Wars* II. 104). As he stood firm, evading javelins or catching them on his shield, his military tribunes ran forward and formed up alongside him. The legions rallied. Caesar later admitted that he had often fought for victory, but on this occasion it was for his life; indeed, when he saw his soldiers retreat, he thought of killing himself.

The situation was finally saved, as on previous occasions, by the Tenth Legion which, from its privileged position on the right of the line, broke up the opposition left wing, and by a brilliant move by Bogud and his cavalry. Thirty thousand Pompeian troops were slaughtered in the fight, including Labienus, who was buried where he lay; all 13 legionary standards were captured. Gnaeus Pompeius fled, but was hunted down and killed; then his head was cut off and publicly displayed in Hispalis. Sextus Pompeius survived.

The battle of Munda took place in March 45 BC. Caesar sorted out to his satisfaction the situation in Spain, with some assistance from Octavius, who arrived in May on his own initiative, too late for the battle but not too late to make himself useful. He then moved on by stages to Narbo, where reception parties from Rome were beginning to attach themselves to his entourage. Among them were Mark Antony and Gaius Trebonius, who shared a tent. Caesar was particularly welcoming to Antony; he promised him the consulship in 44 BC, and invited him to share his carriage for the rest of the journey, relegating Octavius to the carriage behind, with Decimus Brutus.

Caesar, master of Rome, was now master of the Roman empire, and effectively of the world. Mark Antony did not, however, tell Caesar that one night he had been sounded out by Trebonius about taking part in a plot to assassinate him.

BRUTUS

# 10

# THE IDES OF MARCH 44 BC

Cato used to say that Caesar was the only man who attempted
to upset the constitution while sober.

Suetonius, *Julius Caesar* 53

Caesar was having less time now for those who refused to understand what he
was trying to do. When Cicero published a eulogy of Cato, Caesar, while still
in Spain after the battle of Munda, sat down to write a rebuttal, and ordered
Aulus Hirtius to do the same. Hirtius's effort seemed to Cicero so pathetic
that he invited Atticus to publish it as publicity for his own book. Even
Caesar found it hard to combat Cicero's command of eloquence and reason.
His *Anti-Cato* opened with a deft tribute to Cicero, with whose literary
ability he said his own compared so poorly, but, in striving to destroy Cato's
personal reputation, an almost impossible task, Caesar descended to the kind
of personal muck-raking more redolent of the hustings. Yet even while giving vent to his iritation, he was sufficiently sensitive to personal feelings to
send, at the end of April 45 BC, a letter of condolence to Cicero on the death
of his daughter Tullia; she was recently divorced from Dolabella, who never
refunded the dowry.

Having settled some personal business in Italy, Caesar finally returned to
Rome at the beginning of October 45 BC. In the meantime the senate and

139

popular assemblies had been devising further honours for his, and their, gratification. He was granted the permanent title of *imperator*, to be hereditary. For his final victory in Spain he was to be known as the 'Liberator', and an additional temple to Libertas, goddess of freedom, was to be erected in his honour. He was to have a palace built for him on the Quirinal Hill out of public funds. As well as being appointed dictator, he was now also made consul for ten years, with the entire control of the army and of state finance. An ivory statue of Caesar was to be carried along with those of the gods in the procession inaugurating each occasion of the games. A further statue of him was to be set up in the temple of Romulus, founder of Rome, with the inscription, 'To the invincible god', and yet another on the Capitol Hill beside those of the ancient kings of Rome and of Lucius Junius Brutus, who was said to have instigated the rebellion against the monarchy which led to the establishment of the republic. The senate and people of Rome had made Caesar king in all but name, and had in addition conferred on him trappings of divinity.

His enemies regarded such gestures as tactless, if not also distasteful, and registered their disapproval by voting against them in the senate – it is recorded that Caesar did not question their right to do so. He was trying to refine a constitution which had foundered on the jealousies and ambitions of the few with access to power, and to replace it with something that would be more acceptable to new Romans representing disparate peoples of the empire. He was prepared to ignore those who were still not ready to see this. At the same time he was not the kind of person to ignore the investment of his intentions with the mystique of a ruler cult: these were supreme statements of the nature of the *dignitas* which he had aspired to and achieved. During the republic, however, such was the antipathy to monarchy that the word *rex* had the meaning of 'tyrant' as well as of 'king' – Cicero frequently used it in the former sense.

The *optimates* and those sympathetic to their views still staunchly opposed Caesar. There was also a growing number of those who feared him, disliked him, were bewildered by the extent and nature of the sudden changes to their society, or saw in his every action a manifestation of arrogance. Certainly these last were presented with a certain amount of justification for their attitude.

A few days after his return to Rome, Caesar insisted on celebrating a triumph for his Spanish victory over Gnaeus Pompeius, scion of a famous Roman family, and his substantially Roman-citizen troops, something he had diplomatically avoided doing after defeating Gnaeus's father at Pharsalus and the survivors of Pharsalus in Africa. This caused much ill-feeling. There was an incident, described by Suetonius (*Julius Caesar* 78), during the procession; one of the tribunes of the people, Pontius Aquila, remained firmly in his seat as Caesar's chariot passed. Caesar called out to him by name: 'Come on, Aquila, are you using your office to get me to resuscitate the republic?'

He retaliated in his ironic fashion: for several days afterwards, any undertaking was qualified with the words, 'If tribune Aquila pleases!' That said, after the procession he had provided lunch for the public but, having decided that it was not lavish enough, in a demonstration of typical generosity gave another, more elaborate one, five days later.

Caesar also caused offence by breaking with tradition and ordering triumphs for his two commanders in Spain, Fabius Maximus and Quintus Pedius, and by giving up the consulship for the final three months of 45 BC in favour of Fabius and Gaius Trebonius. To recognize publicly the contribution of subordinates to a military campaign is a sign of an enlightened leader. By resigning as consul in favour of a *consul suffectus* for the rest of the year, he instituted a constructive precedent of which Roman emperors who ruled after him, and who in the same way as Caesar accepted continuous consulships, took constitutional advantage: there could now be more public administrators with experience at the highest level available for significant posts abroad.

At some point Caesar had envisaged the necessity of a war in the east, finally to destroy the continuing threat from Parthia to Roman interests in the region and at the same time to lay to rest memories of the disaster at Carrhae and the manner of the death of Crassus. Though he was now 55 and no longer in perfect health, he announced that he would himself lead the campaign, which would begin in 44 BC. Suetonius, as we have seen, records that Caesar twice had an epileptic fit while on military campaign. From cross references to other accounts, these could have been at Thapsus in 46 and at Corduba in 45 BC. There is no reason to doubt the diagnosis, nor any reason to give the condition a fancy name such as temporal lobe epilepsy. One does not need to be born with epilepsy to develop it late in life, only to have a lower than normal seizure threshold; an attack can be brought on by nothing more unusual than stress. It is most unlikely that Caesar suffered from epilepsy all his life. The condition was at the time hedged round with such superstition that this would have been mentioned somewhere. It is also improbable that anyone suffering from epilepsy would have been elected or appointed to high religious office in Rome; if there were any break in a ritual, such as could happen if a participant had the most minor of seizures, the whole process had to be gone through again from the beginning. The instances of Caesar's seizures are consistent with the condition now recognized simply as late onset epilepsy, for which often no cause is identifiable. To Caesar, however, without benefit of modern science, they could have seemed to presage death.

The prospective Parthian campaign was reflected in the appointment of senior officials for subsequent years. Mark Antony, as he had been promised, was chosen consul for 44 BC; Caesar would be his consular colleague until he left for Parthia, when Dolabella (who according to Appian was only 25) would replace him. Fourteen praetors and 40 quaestors were elected for 44.

For 43 BC, when the consuls would be Aulus Hirtius and Gaius Vibius Pansa, there were to be 16 praetors; Cassius Dio remarks that there was no other way that Caesar could stand by his additional promises. When the new tribunes took office in December 45 BC, Lucius Antonius (brother of Mark Antony) had a measure passed which gave Caesar the right to nominate half the candidates for all offices of state except the consulship – according to Cassius Dio, this turned out to mean that he nominated all of them. In addition to his being formally appointed by popular vote commander of the Parthian expedition, Caesar was authorized to choose officials for the three additional years 43–41 BC which the campaign was expected to last. In his capacity as dictator Caesar appointed Octavius to replace Lepidus as master of the cavalry from when the expedition should leave until the end of 44 BC. In the meantime Octavius had been dispatched to Apollonia to further his military studies among the legions stationed in Macedonia. While acting only marginally outside his constitutional rights, Caesar, in the interests of effective administration, had finally destroyed the republican tradition of free elections.

Even Caesar, however, sometimes took a break from the fervour of his official business. His niece Atia, mother of Octavius and Octavia, had married, as her second husband, Lucius Marcius Philippus, who owned a villa near Puteoli. Marcius Philippus had been consul in 56 BC, but took no part in the civil wars. Caesar went to stay with them on the day after the festival of Saturnalia in December, accompanied by an entourage of 2000, including a troop of armed cavalry. The next afternoon he went over to call on Cicero in one of the latter's several country houses. Cicero was obliged to ask one of his friends to lend him the necessary security guards, and had not only to give dinner to his distinguished guest, but also to feed his immediate attendants in three other dining-rooms. Though Caesar was famously abstemious, on this occasion he was taking emetics, and indulged with considerable enjoyment. In a letter to Atticus, Cicero admitted that he quite enjoyed the occasion, but that Caesar was not the kind of guest to whom one says, 'Do come again next time you are in this area,' adding, ' "Once is enough" ' (*To Atticus* XIII. 52).

On his return to Rome, Caesar faced further rounds of accolades from the senate. He was granted the designation of *pater patriae* (father of the country). In addition to his title of *imperator*, his office of *pontifex maximus* was also made hereditary, should he have or adopt a son. His terms as dictator and 'Controller of Public Morals' were extended to cover his life, and both he and any son of his were awarded permanently the same inviolability that applied to tribunes of the people.

On another occasion they conferred on him, with only a handful of objectors, privileges usually reserved for a god, including the dedication of a new temple to him and Clementia, the personification of his attribute of clemency, with Mark Antony as their special priest. The measures were to be

*Figure 10.1* Silver *denarius* of 44 BC, the first Roman coin to depict a living person. The inscription (obverse) is CAESAR. IMP., with, behind the head, the curved staff of an augur. On the reverse, an armed Venus holds a figure of victory, below which is a sceptre. The name M. Mettius is that of the moneyer. (× 2)

inscribed in gold on tablets of silver. Then the whole senate, headed by the suffect consuls and the state officials, processed to the Forum Julium to give Caesar the good news. They found him in the vestibule of the temple of Venus Genetrix, where he received them without rising from his chair. All the ancient writers who describe this incident are agreed that this was an offence against protocol of the first magnitude, resented not just by his enemies, but also by the senate in general and by members of the public. The details are as instructive as they are varied.

The historian Nicolaus of Damascus, who was about 20 years old at the time, says that Caesar was so busy conducting business with those around him that he did not notice the approach of the deputation until it was pointed out to him. Then he simply put down his papers and turned to listen. Appian suggests that his remaining seated was deliberate, and that this gave his detractors justification for believing that he wished to be approached as though he were king. Suetonius, who was a professional archivist, records that according to some accounts Caesar was getting to his feet when Balbus stopped him; but that, according to others, he did nothing of the kind, and when his legal adviser, Gaius Trebatius Testa, motioned to him to stand up, he simply glared back at him. Plutarch repeats the reference to Balbus restraining him, but adds that Caesar, as though he were dealing with members of the public, suggested that the honours might be scaled down, which caused further offence. Then, realizing he had committed a faux pas, on his way out he drew back the folds of his toga from his neck and cried out to his friends that he was offering his throat to anyone who wanted to kill him. Afterwards, he issued a statement which cited his medical condition as the reason for his behaviour, claiming that those who suffered from it could not stand up to address a crowd without feeling giddy. Cassius Dio recounts that Caesar's apologists tried to excuse him on the grounds that he was having an attack of diarrhoea and could not rise in case he was taken short; they obviously did not see him, soon afterwards, get to his feet and walk home.

The annalists had another field day describing the events of the last day of 45 BC. At 7 o'clock in the morning, members of the tribal assembly gathered on the Campus Martius to elect the quaestors for the following year. Caesar had taken the auspices when it was announced that the consul Fabius Maximus had died suddenly. Fabius's chair of office was removed. Caesar, assuming the function of *interrex*, instead of appointing another suffect consul for the rest of the day or carrying on without one, had the meeting reorganize itself into centuries, convened a *comitia centuriata*, and conducted an election for a consul to hold office until the next morning. Gaius Caninius Rebilius, one of Caesar's former legates, was duly elected. Though Cicero joked that Caninius was so assiduous in his duties that he never closed his eyes during the whole of his consulship, and that during Caninius's consulship no-one ate breakfast, died-in-the-wool republicans, such as Cicero was himself, regarded Caesar's actions that day as further devaluing traditional institutions of state.

Caesar was not the kind of reformer who carried others along with him. It was not a case of 'we can do it more effectively' so much as 'I can do it more effectively'. He was recreating the constitution in his own image, consciously or subconsciously moulding a system which required one man in overall control, if anyone after him should emerge who was up to the job. He was rebuilding the empire into a more cohesive body by enfranchising Italy, bringing provincials into the senate, reorganizing the provincial system itself, encouraging self-government, and establishing Roman colonies overseas, of which the significant new foundations at Carthage and Corinth can both be dated to 44 BC, while his earlier addition to the empire of Gaul ensured that for several hundred years there was a buffer between Italy and the dangerously volatile Germanic and other tribal groupings to the east.

It was not, however, his manipulation of the constitution or even his elevation to the status of a divinity that caused the greatest resentment, so much as his ambivalent attitude to those who wished actually to dub him 'king'. Caesar would go through the motions of denying the title, even to the extent of rebuking those who linked him with it, but without showing any genuine displeasure at the notion. It was thus perhaps inevitable that someone should place a crown on one of his public statues. Two of the tribunes, Gaius Epidius Marullus and Lucius Caesetius Flavus, removed it on the grounds that Caesar did not want anything of the kind. On 26 January 44 BC, while Caesar was returning on horseback from celebrating a religious festival on the Alban Mount, which overlooks Aricia, spectators called out to him as king. To which Caesar responded, ' "My name is not King; it is Caesar' " (Plutarch, *Julius Caesar* 60), pretending to misinterpret the message. When this attempt at a witticism fell flat with the crowd, he angrily rode on.